Bad Grammar and Brass Monkeys

How to improve your bloody grammar and writing skills

RICHARD HEAGY, J.D.

Bad Grammar and Brass Monkeys

Published by Northfleet Publishers
[an imprint of Northfleet Group LLC]

ISBN - 13: 978-0-692-76825-9

TABLE OF CONTENTS

1   Commonly Misunderstood Definitions
2   Who is this Book for?
3   What is the Purpose of this Book?
4   British vs American Usage
5   Following Instructions
6   More About Following Instructions – University Style
    Requirements
7   Proofreading
8   Spell Checks
9   Grammar Checks
10 Do I have to Avoid Bad Grammar Completely?
11 What about Partial Sentences?
12 Use of Standard English
13 Keep it Formal
14 Formatting
15 Cutting and Pasting
16 Inconsistency
17 Presentation and First Impressions
18 What's Next?
19 Writing Style – Variety
20 What is a Sentence?
21 Are all of your Sentences the Same?
22 Sentence Fragments
23 Starting a Sentence with a Coordinating Conjunction
24 Unfinished Sentences vs Sentence Fragments
25 Parenthetical Expressions
26 Punctuation Marks
27 Commas
28 Semicolons
29 Commas vs Semicolons
30 Colons
31 Apostrophes
32 Question Marks
33 Full Stops (Periods)
34 Capitalisation
35 Capitalisation and Punctuation – Lists and Headings
36 Quotation Marks
37 Citations and Statistics
38 Italics
39 Emphasis
40 Separate or Combined Words

41   Either Combined or Separate Words may be Correct
42   Hyphens
43   Prefixes
44   Numbers
45   Words Existing in Singular Form Only
46   Commonly Confused Words – Same Sound
47   Commonly Confused Words – Similar Sound
48   Wrong Word Choice
49   Wrong Combinations
50   Misused Words
51   Other Word Choices
52   Words with More than One Meaning
53   ETCETERA (ETC.)
54   Parallel Construction
55   Shifting Tenses
56   Subject/Verb Agreement – Plural and Singular
57   Noun/Pronoun Agreement
58   Faulty Predication
59   Faulty Coordination
60   Active vs Passive Voice in Sentences
61   Run-on-Sentences
62   Wordy Sentences and Phrases
63   Redundancy
64   Words and Other Things to Avoid
65   Missing Articles
66   Hotchpotch
67   Logical Writing
68   Queue Properly
69   Did You Write What You Meant to Say?
70   Can You Improve?
71   How to Start Writing
72   Style of Writing
73   Proofread, Edit and Criticise Your Own Work
74   Proofreading, Editing and Rewriting
75   Editing and Rewriting – Do it More than Once
76   Filler Material
77   Waffle Paragraphs
78   Use an Axe to Tighten Up Your Work
79   Brevity
80   Reorganizing Word Order
81   Ambiguity and Confusion
82   Mistakes Frequently Found in Student Essays
83   Conclusion

Bad Grammar and Brass Monkeys

How to improve your bloody grammar and writing skills

'Brass monkey' is a colloquialism used to indicate extremely cold temperatures. Its use and exact meaning have changed over the centuries, with different versions from various sources. The more recent version, from the 20th century, used by some English speakers nowadays is 'cold enough to freeze the balls off a brass monkey'. It's time for you to come in out of the cold and leave your grammar, spelling and punctuation problems behind.

Are you tired of working your arse off to all hours of the night, barely turning in your masterpiece at the last minute, only to wait for eternity (it seems) for your grades while the instructor may be on holiday, and then to have your composition returned with unkind comments?

Wait, where's the grade? It must be here somewhere: an A or a B; maybe a C; no it can't be. You are gobsmacked. How about a few choice words for the professor, and maybe the lecturer; while you're at it, why not throw in the caretaker? 'Bollocks' for starters.

There must be a better way, other than buying a thick book on grammar and punctuation that would only end up functioning as a doorstop. Doing the laundry would probably be more pleasant, and you can't afford another expensive textbook in any event.

WAIT!

You don't have to make a career out of grammar and punctuation. You have already made a career choice; and it bloody hell wasn't English grammar or you would not be reading this book.

All you need is a little help, a few tips on how to avoid the most common mistakes that will prevent your composition from being another pile of tosh. Although we will be teaching you how to improve your grammar, a bit of British slang thrown in here and there should occasionally lighten the experience.

Do you know what the following terms mean?

Alliteration
Conjunction
Comma Splice
Double negative
Hyperbole
Prepositional phrase

If so, this book is not for you, and thank you for buying it anyway. Don't get cheesed off over a few pounds; give it to a friend or a fellow student.

Let's test your knowledge before proceeding:

What is the difference between a dangling participle and a dangling modifier? You don't want to know. If you have either one, see your doctor immediately and have it removed.

COMMONLY MISUNDERSTOOD DEFINITIONS

A proper noun – does not actually refer to a graduate of Oxford or Cambridge.

Aphorism – something that usually goes away in a few days if treated promptly.

Appositives – something you insert in your . . . never mind.

Comma splice – call your TV repairman.

Conjunctive adverb – your eye doctor can remove this with a simple procedure.

Coordinating conjunctive – two procedures done at the same time while on the operating table.

Dangling modifier – something that should be removed from the body as soon as possible.

Gerund – the English gerund usually has an 'ing' ending, but not all endings are that pleasant.

Hyphens – do not use hyphens in adjectives as it turns them mouldy within three days.

Predicate – a word that could get you in trouble if used in public.

Present participle – something you do not want in your body.

Split infinitive – can be fixed up with a few stitches.

Cobblers, you say, and rightly so. Just a little humour before we delve—not too deeply—into the heavy stuff. If you want to know what the foregoing terms mean, you will have to look them up.

WHO IS THIS BOOK FOR?

This book was initially designed for UK University students at all levels, even graduate students. However, it is equally useful for lower-level students, as well as users of American English. It is *not* primarily for the benefit of students whose first language is not English, although they may benefit more than native English speakers. Although certain types of mistakes are more likely to be made by non-native speakers, such mistakes are frequently made by native English speakers as well; most of the advice contained in this book will benefit all students, whatever their native language, and improve their grammar, punctuation and writing skills.

WHAT IS THE PURPOSE OF THIS BOOK?

The purpose of this book is to improve your writing by reducing many of the types of mistakes frequently found in the work of university students, not to teach you all the rules of grammar. It is a practical guide rather than a grammar or punctuation text, although these topics are covered to the extent deemed useful, as well as suggestions on how to enhance the quality of your writing skills. The goal is to improve your work, and move it closer to an academic standard, but you have to want to improve and put in a bit of effort. Even though Albert Einstein said *'Never memorize something that you can look up'*, you still need to understand some basic rules. If you forget whether to put the name of a book, movie title or magazine article in quotation marks or italics, you can look it up, although we will tell you what to use later on.

BRITISH vs AMERICAN USAGE

The focus of this book is grammar, punctuation and academic writing skills for UK university students. You will come across writing from time to time that does not appear to be in accordance with the rules of proper British grammar, but may instead have been written according to American rules. In many cases both British and American examples are given so that you will know the difference when you see them. In a given case greater clarity may be achieved with American usage, often with more commas. In addition to grammar differences, several words are spelt differently in American English. UK/US examples: analyse/analyze; centre/center; colour/color; defence/defense; emphasise/emphasize; grey/gray; kerb/curb; labour/labor; licence/license; mum/mom; offence/offense; organise/organize; tyre/tire; towards/toward; traveller/traveler; and aluminium/aluminium, which is mentioned as it is used later on.

FOLLOWING INSTRUCTIONS

Maybe you are the kind of person who buys a coffee grinder or other appliance and jumps right in, using it without reading the instructions, at least until it stops working. Bad news for you as that will not work for academic papers or university presentations.

You must read the instructions of your assignment carefully before you start, and again after you have finished writing. You may have missed something: one or more sections, answering a question, or failing to place the required information in a template. Present the content in the proper order, usually in the order listed in the assignment.

Section titles, if used, should be worded to accurately describe what the reader will find in each section. If you cannot figure out a good title for a section, there is probably something wrong with what you wrote. The last thing you want is for the person reading and marking your work to find it confusing. That person has probably already started on his or her task of marking other students' submissions for the class, and by now may be in a foul mood, depending on the quality, or often lack of quality, of the submissions reviewed thus far.

Failing to follow instructions in writing essays is a frequent failing of students. If you are asked to analyse the current state of the music industry and your project's place in it, don't merely discuss the music industry in general terms, followed by a brief description of your project. You must analyse the current state of the industry; then explain how your project fits into the industry. Stay focused, stick to the topic and exclude extraneous material.

Another failing of students is failure to justify conclusions or choices. Going back to the preceding example, your assignment may also require that you choose a career in the music industry, explain the steps that you will take to become successful and justify your choices. If you leave out the last item (justify your choices) you are in trouble. Academic work often requires more than just an informative discussion of a topic; you may be required to analyse or justify. Following the instructions means more than proper formatting. Unfortunately it means work; often a lot of work.

If you are given two related assignments about a topic, such as a business plan and a contextual essay, treat each as an independent document and follow the instructions for each one very carefully. Because the documents cover similar material, students sometimes leave something out of one of the documents or omit material from a discussion that is included in the other paper. This is easy to do because all of the information is in your head and you may not realise that you have failed to get something down on paper in both documents. Each of your writings will be judged on its own and must be complete.

MORE ABOUT FOLLOWING INSTRUCTIONS – UNVERSITY STYLE REQUIREMENTS

Your university may require that you conform to a particular style manual for your writing, such as *The Chicago Manual of Style, The Associated Press Handbook*, or the *MHRA Style Guide*. Many universities have their own style guides, which generally apply to university staff, publications and websites, not academic writing of students. You must read your university's style requirements carefully to determine what rules apply to academic writing, but it may not be that simple. The University of Kent, for example, lists (separately for each college) several style guides that may be used. Using the proper style manual or guide is part of following instructions, whether or not mentioned by your instructor or in the class assignment. You will have to look elsewhere, and should already have done that. Following a particular style manual may require that you deviate from the advice in this book in a given case; however, most of the remaining content of this book will remain applicable and improve your writing.

PROOFREADING

Even if you learn all of the rules explained in this book, you will not be successful unless you proofread your work. This requires more than just doing a spelling and grammar check on the computer, which will not reveal mistakes such as inconsistent spacing and font types or other formatting problems. Technically 'font' refers to the computer program that tells a computer or printer how to display characters, whereas 'typeface; (e.g., Times New Roman) refers to the way a group of letters or numbers appear. Because most people refer to typefaces as fonts, we will use the term 'font' for convenience. The eye does not catch all mistakes on the computer screen. Not everything pops out at you. A final proofreading should consist of reading over your material in hard copy, red marking pen in hand. You may be surprised at what you missed by proofreading on the computer screen. Final proofreading is best done in a nearby coffeehouse. A pub may be tempting as an alternative, but...

SPELL CHECKS

Some errors are not really spelling errors, but merely *typos* where you inadvertently hit the wrong letter on the keyboard. These are usually underlined in red and thus may be corrected promptly, even before a spell check is done. However, if your typo results in something that is in fact a word, but not the one you intended, a spellchecker will not spot the problem, and a grammar check may or may not, depending on the error.

EX: He always *had* a habit of studying at the last minute. [correct]

EX: He always *bad* a habit of studying at the last minute. [incorrect]

NOTE: The spellchecker will not show that you have typed the wrong word. Depending on your software, the incorrect sentence may or may not be underlined in green to indicate a grammar mistake, which is not the problem. This is why you must proofread carefully from a hard copy.

Note that some software programs combine the spell and grammar checks, while others do them separately. You should first verify that the language of your software program is set for British English, unless you intend to use American English. See comments under EDITING AND REWRITING – DO IT MORE THAN ONCE.

GRAMMAR CHECKS

Grammar seems to be a bigger problem than spelling for university students in writing essays, with punctuation being a close second. Although a grammar check will give you different results depending on the word processing program you are using, the work of many students indicates that a grammar check was not even attempted. For example, Microsoft Word may show you fewer errors or suggestions than Word Perfect, but this usually results from the default settings. In Microsoft Word the default is usually set on <u>Grammar Only</u>, which will correct spelling and minimal grammar problems. If you select <u>Grammar and Style</u> instead, you will notice quite a difference in suggested changes and corrections. No matter what program you use, the suggestions will not always be correct or applicable. If your material contains a large amount of dialog, which is often one sentence in the case of fiction, the comment that a paragraph consists of more than one sentence is not helpful or appropriate and becomes tedious after a while. You should investigate various software programs and test them by comparing the results of grammar checks using the same sentence or paragraph. In comparing programs, it is necessary to look at the settings as the results of a grammar check may differ widely (even within the same program).

DO I HAVE TO AVOID BAD GRAMMAR COMPLETELY?

Bad grammar may be used to quote what a character actually says in a novel or screenplay or other narrative; other than that, it has no place in academic work and should be avoided.

WHAT ABOUT PARTIAL SENTENCES?

The use of a few words that do not constitute a complete sentence, including sentence fragments, should be reserved for narrative descriptions, instructions, and dialogue in screenplays or novels. Other than that, they should not appear in academic work. See the discussion below under <u>UNFINISHED</u> <u>SENTENCES vs SENTENCE FRAGMENTS</u>.

USE OF STANDARD ENGLISH

Many words, such as 'conversate', which will be underlined in red if you are using Microsoft Word, are considered to be words by some, but are not 'standard English' and may give your instructor a jolt or a strong headache. You should stick to *Standard English* for academic work. Slang should be avoided unless appropriate, and is used in this book on occasion merely to give you a brief reprieve from the book's heavy-duty subject matter.

EX: How many kids do you think will come to the concert? [slang]
EX: How many children do you think will come to the concert? [standard/formal]

EX: You should mail the invites for the party by Friday. [slang]
EX: You should mail the invitations for the party by Friday. [standard/formal]

Word usage, grammar and spelling have changed over the centuries and picked up speed in recent decades. Changes are generally acceptable more rapidly in informal rather than academic usage, and even more so in spoken English. The different spelling of words sometimes put forth by a diverse number of dictionaries does not make life easy for a writer. This is apart from the occasional differences in spelling between American and British English. Even the use of punctuation is not entirely free of differing opinions. In this book, we have selected the usage that we consider most appropriate for academic writing. If you use other sources that contradict our advice, you should first determine whether or not such sources are focused on academic writing or merely on general usage before you decide what to do.

KEEP IT FORMAL

Keep your writing formal for academic work, not the way you or characters in a novel speak. Avoid contractions, colloquial expressions, slang and abbreviations.

> SLANG: I thought I was gonna get a B in maths, but I watched TV all weekend before the final exam and got a D.

> FORMAL: I thought I was going to receive a B in maths, but I watched television all weekend before the final exam and received a D.

You should also avoid the use of personal pronouns (*I, me, my*) in academic work, which then will make your work appear more objective.

> EX: I believe that universities in the United Kingdom should reduce tuition. [avoid]

> EX: Universities in the United Kingdom should reduce tuition. [better]

> NOTE: Be careful with the use or omission of that. There is no difference in meaning in the two examples which follow. However, the omission of that is not acceptable for academic writing even though its omission in speaking is common.

> EX: I decided that maths was too difficult and dropped the class. [academic]
> EX: I decided maths was too difficult and dropped the class. [informal]

Informal grammar is frequently used by people when they speak. It is not only used in the speech of fictional characters in a novel, but frequently in the narrative of a fictional work as well. Academic work, on the other hand, must be restricted to proper grammar. In addition to speech, informal writing and formal (including academic) writing, there is another style for news.

FORMATTING

Proper formatting is necessary to give your work a professional look. Follow any requirements of your university or instructions in your assignment as to formatting. If a template is required, use it. Several things will give your work a sloppy appearance and immediately detract from the content, as brilliant as it may be, including the following, which appear too often in student work:

- Cramming paragraphs together without adequate space between them (usually one line)
- Leaving a space between the last word in a sentence and the full stop
- Using different types of fonts
- Using different font sizes (see exception below)
- Using bold inconsistently (e.g., some paragraph headings in bold, others not)
- Centre alignment, especially when mixed with left alignment
- Lists of items with sloppy alignment
- Bullet points not lined up
- Capitalizing some, but not all, items in a list
- Capitalizing the first word of some, but not all, sentences

Exception for font sizes: Sometimes the use of the same size font for a heading that is in bold will result in a heavy look; using a font one size smaller may look better for the bold heading, as shown by the following examples.

| **SAMPLE HEADING** | [size 10] |
| Content under the heading. | [size 10] |

| **SAMPLE HEADING** | [size 9] |
| Content under the heading. | [size 10] |

CUTTING AND PASTING

Cutting and pasting may result in a different font appearing out of nowhere, destroying the otherwise nicely formatted look to a page. This is not the only problem that can result. The material copied may have an extra word or one or more words missing, or may be pasted in the wrong place. After you cut and paste, read the entire paragraph where you pasted the material again to see if it fits smoothly into the sentence or paragraph; grammar or punctuation changes may be necessary. Then reread the paragraph where the cut material came from to see if it still makes sense and that the flow of information is not interrupted.

INCONSISTENCY

Some items of inconsistent use are related to formatting and include

- Using different types of fonts
- Using different font sizes (see exception above under FORMATTING)
- Using bold inconsistently (e.g., some paragraph headings in bold, others not)
- Centre alignment mixed with left alignment
- Lists of items with sloppy alignment
- Capitalizing some, but not all, items in a list
- Capitalizing the first word of some, but not all, sentences

Other items of inconsistent use that give your work a sloppy look include the following:

- Proper names in the middle of a sentence sometimes capitalized, and other times not
- The same word spelt inconsistently throughout the document
- Two words combined as a single word, and in other places used as separate words
  - E.g., teammate, and team mate
  - Even if you use the wrong spelling consistently, it looks better than mixing it up
- Similarly, two words used as a single word, and in other places joined with a hyphen (again, be consistent even if you are wrong)
- To make matters more difficult, some compound words may be used as separate words, combined as a single word, or joined together with a hyphen, so you have to make a choice, but once made, be consistent.

The content of your essay should be consistent. For example, do not say in the middle of your music business essay that a band should incorporate as a company or limited liability partnership in order to avoid personal liability and later on state that you will form a band as a general partnership (which will not avoid personal liability).

PRESENTATION AND FIRST IMPRESSIONS

First impressions are always important, whether you are applying for a job or submitting your academic paper to your instructor. If your formatting looks clean and professional, you are off to a good start. This good impression will continue, at least for a while, if your first paragraph is well written. The bad news is that you may go downhill from then on if the reading of your material discloses misplaced commas, grammatical gaffs, run-on sentences, missing semicolons and awkward wording. Hopefully that will not be the case as you will have followed the advice in this book and will have complied with all of the requirements of your assignment.

Another warning—the worst thing that can happen (other than misspelling the instructor's name) is for the reader to turn the page and find a paragraph that fills the whole page without any breaks. That is when the reader will rub his or her eyes and say 'Bollocks' or something worse. You must avoid extremely long paragraphs at all cost. They should never be longer than a few sentences. If you have diligently read a paragraph to the bottom of the page non-stop, you must go back and split the paragraph up into several shorter
paragraphs, which should vary in length, as discussed later on. This may also require some rewriting and some effort. The worst formatting, not unknown in student work, is an entire essay with no spaces between paragraphs.

WHAT'S NEXT?

Now that we have explained how to make your work look presentable, it is time to improve your writing with respect to grammar, punctuation and usage, not the quality of the content, which is up to you. The following rules are not presented in any particular order of importance. You will not be given a long list of definitions to memorize. Instead, we will show you common mistakes frequently made by students, with examples, and how to avoid them. Even though some rules are rather straightforward, examples are often given merely to show you how awful incorrect writing looks, and what you instructor might see if you are not careful. The cliché 'A picture is worth a thousand words' can be applied to examples, so we have been generous.

WRITING STYLE - VARIETY

Before we start; a few comments about style. Paragraphs, as mentioned above, should never take up a full page. Paragraph length should vary throughout your work. This will affect the flow of your work and its readability. Instructors will nod off less often while reading it. The same is true of sentences, which should vary in length, long and short. This does not mean that every other sentence should be long or short, only that there be variation overall. Short sentences will not all be the same length, and neither will long ones. Extremely long sentences, though grammatically correct, will affect readability and should be rewritten as more than one sentence.

Repetition must be avoided as it will bore the reader and reflect poor writing style. Avoid starting too many sentences with the same word, especially two consecutive sentences. This includes, for example, overuse of the word *The* or *It* to begin a sentence. Try not to use the same word two or more times in the same sentence. You can resolve these problems with the use of synonyms or using pronouns in place of nouns. If there is no alternative, change the word order instead of starting two consecutive sentences with the same word. This may take a little work, but is worth the effort.

Pronouns—words that take the place of nouns (persons, places and things)—can also be used to avoid repetition within a sentence.

EX: After Michael turned in Michael's essay, it was too late to proofread the essay one more time.
EX: After *Michael* turned in *his* essay, it was too late to proofread *it* one more time.

NOTE: In the second example repetition is avoided by substituting *his* for *Michael* the second time *Michael* is mentioned, and *it* for *essay* the second time *essay* is mentioned.

EX: The movie was much too long and the movie was not worth £10.

EX: The *movie* was much too long and *it* was not worth £10.

Pronouns can also be used to avoid repetition by alternating from one sentence to the next.

EX: Michael was never late to class until last Monday. For the first time he overslept and did not arrive until noon. The next day Michael bought a new alarm clock.

Do not use a pronoun in place of someone's name if his or her name has not been mentioned for several paragraphs. For example, you might mention Michael as an actor in a movie; then write several paragraphs which do not mention him at all. The next time you mention him use *Michael*, not *he*. It must be clear to the reader who you are talking about.

Words such as *However* and *For example*, which are often used to start a sentence, may be placed later in the sentence for more variation.

EX: However, you should not wait until the last minute to start your paper.

EX: The first draft of my composition on the EU, however, is much too short.

Variation should also be considered in the structure of verb usage, particularly tense (past, present and future) and voice (active and passive). Although this is contrary to the advice to avoid using the passive voice where possible in academic work, the use of the passive voice for variation may be appropriate in some cases.

EX: The Prime Minister will call for an election next year.
EX: The Prime Minister called for an election next year.
EX: The Prime Minister has called for an election next year.

NOTE: The choice of which example to use will depend on the wording of the rest of the paragraph in which the sentence is used.

WHAT IS A SENTENCE?

Merriam-Webster defines a sentence as follows: 'a word, clause, or phrase or a group of clauses or phrases forming a syntactic unit which expresses an assertion, a question, a command, a wish, an exclamation, or the performance of an action, that in writing usually begins with a capital letter and concludes with appropriate end punctuation, and that in speaking is distinguished by characteristic patterns of stress, pitch, and pauses.'
http://www.merriam-webster.com/dictionary/sentence

Rather long-winded; since we are trying to teach brevity, among other things, let's try another definition.

The *Cambridge Dictionaries Online* defines a sentence as 'a group of words, usually containing a subject and a verb, expressing a statement, question, instruction, exclamation, and, when written, starting with a capital letter and ending with a period or other mark.'

Although an over simplification, let's just say for now that a sentence should start with a capital letter and end with a full stop, with something in between, even a single word.

ARE ALL OF YOUR SENTENCES THE SAME?

If all of your sentences are the same the reader will be totally bored and may give up reading long before reaching the end. Sentence length and style should vary to avoid monotony, and the same applies to paragraphs. To start with, don't put too much information or too many ideas in a sentence. A short sentence is often used to set forth an important idea or statement, followed by a longer sentence which supports or expands on the idea or statement.

Varying sentence length between long and short ones is an overall concept and does not mean that you cannot have two consecutive long sentences or two consecutive short sentences.

The goal of varying sentence length is to improve readability. It is a matter of style, not grammar.

There is more than one way to say something, and in fact there are four basic sentence types that you can use to give your work variety. Following is an example of each type, which we will be kind enough not to name.

EX: I would like to leave class early today and go to the cinema.
EX: I am bored with class today, and I would like to leave early and go to the cinema.
EX: Because I am bored with class today, I would like to leave early and go to the cinema.
EX: I am bored with class today because the substitute instructor is not very good, and I would like to leave early and go to the cinema.

The basic word order of a sentence is subject, verb and object, but this order may be moved around to better reflect the desired flow of information or for emphasis or contrast.

EX: Spencer is always the first employee to arrive at work.
EX: The first employee to arrive at work is always Spencer.
EX: It is Spencer who is always the first employee to arrive at work.
EX: It is not any other employee, but Spencer who always arrives at work first.
EX: Try as they might, the other employees could never arrive before Spencer.

In seeking variety in sentence types and word order, remember that you are writing an academic work and anything which detracts from that goal should be avoided. Also, be aware that changing the basic word order may change the meaning of the sentence.

EX: I had my flat painted before my parents came to visit. [Someone else painted it.]
EX: I had painted my flat before my parents came to visit. [I painted it.]

SENTENCE FRAGMENTS

Full stops are also used at the end of sentence fragments, which are not really complete sentences standing by themselves, and should be avoided in academic writing. You can think of a sentence fragment as a partial sentence, or maybe just a phrase, which you may be able to combine with either the sentence preceding or following it. If not, you must rewrite it as a complete sentence. There are many types of sentence fragments, which we will not bore you with since you should not use them in academic writing. The only exception is that you may use a sentence fragment in academic work if it consists of dialogue that you are quoting.

EX: By itself, 'Watching the TV' is a sentence fragment, but 'Watching the TV' would be correct usage (if in quotation marks) in answer to the question 'What are you doing'?

However, one type of sentence fragment should be mentioned as it often appears in students' academic work and is easily remedied, a fragment that is an afterthought which clarifies earlier information in the preceding sentence. If may be possible to add the fragment to the preceding sentence, which sometimes requires the insertion of a comma. In other cases slight rewording may be necessary or the addition of conjunctions, such as *and, but, for, or, nor* or *so,* may be required.

EX: Cinemas usually start with several minutes of advertising before they begin the feature film. A good reason not to arrive on time.

If you are reasonably alert while doing your proofreading, you should be able to see that 'A good reason not to arrive on time' is not a complete sentence. Suggested possible revisions are as follows:

EX: Cinemas usually start with several minutes of advertising before they begin the feature film, which is a good reason not to arrive on time.

EX: Cinemas usually start with several minutes of advertising before they begin the feature film, a good reason not to arrive on time.

Don't forget that after a full stop the next sentence starts with the first word capitalised. If not, maybe you meant to use a comma. Look at your work—carefully.

STARTING A SENTENCE WITH A COORDINATING CONJUNCTION

Conjunctions link two parts of a sentence in order to connect two thoughts or ideas, either with or without a comma between them (as appropriate).

EX: I went to class every day and was never late.
EX: The instructor promised to give me a C if I did not miss any classes, but he didn't.

You could divide the above example into two sentences, starting the second with a coordinating conjunction (*But*) for more emphasis.

EX: The instructor promised to give me a C if I did not miss any classes. But he didn't.

It is generally agreed that the 'rule' against starting a sentence with a coordinating conjunction (and, but, for, nor, or, so, yet) is a myth. However, you cannot start a sentence with a coordinating conjunction if the words that follow are merely a sentence fragment and cannot stand alone as a complete sentence.

EX: The book was interesting. But not well-written.
[incorrect: a sentence fragment]
EX: The book was interesting, but not well-written. [correct]

In addition to emphasis, a sentence may be started with a coordinating conjunction as an afterthought to the previous sentence.

EX: I went to a karaoke bar with my friends last week and they invited me again. But once is enough. [non-academic: use of a sentence fragment for emphasis and as an afterthought]

Starting sentences with a coordinating conjunction should be limited, particularly in academic writing. Such sentences will usually interrupt smooth reading much less if kept short.

UNFINISHED SENTENCES vs SENTENCE FRAGMENTS

Another problem students sometimes have is leaving sentences unfinished, either ending them abruptly with a full stop or just leaving a blank space (generally at the end of a paragraph). This is not the same as intentionally using a sentence fragment, and is not that uncommon. It often results from the student being interrupted or distracted in the middle of a sentence and not picking up where he or she left off, although this is not always the case.

A sentence fragment, though not a complete sentence, often adds additional information or commentary with respect to the preceding sentence, and can often be attached to it without rewording. An incomplete sentence may not have any relationship to the preceding sentence and cannot be attached as a continuation of the preceding sentence as is. It will appear to be a separate sentence that merely stopped abruptly mid-point; it starts expressing a thought that is not completed.

EX: I completed all of my goals during my first year at university. Studying though not something I was interested in.

NOTE: Although this may look like a sentence fragment, it should not be considered as such because it appears more like an unfinished sentence. With a bit of work you could do some rewriting and combine the two into a single sentence, or just complete the unfinished sentence.

PARENTHETICAL EXPRESSIONS

Commas are generally used to set off parenthetical expressions, but parentheses or dashes may also be used (as discussed below). For purposes of this book, the term 'parenthetical expressions' includes any expressions, phrases, words, descriptions, explanations or comments that interrupt the sentence. They add information or commentary but are not essential for making sentences complete. Although often found in the middle, a parenthetical can also be used to start or end a sentence. Do not omit the second comma at the end of a parenthetical expression which is in the middle of a sentence. Either use two commas or none in such cases, as appropriate;

parenthetical expressions which begin or end a sentence only require one comma.

Essential and non-essential clauses

The rule for enclosing parenthetical expressions between commas applies only if you can delete the expression from the sentence without changing its connotation—what you are trying to say. If not, leave the words in but do not insert commas. If you are unsure what to do, try writing the sentence without the parenthetical and see if the sentence still works as a complete thought, without any essential information missing. If it does not sound right, you now know what to do.

EX: He said my composition, which ran over thirty pages, was too long.

NOTE: ['which ran over thirty pages' is non-essential information, and if deleted the sentence reads as follows: 'He said my composition was too long.' Thus, the commas are properly used in the example.]

NOTE FURTHER: [Although some sentences may be punctuated either with or without commas, the meaning would be different.]

EX: The students drinking strong coffee finished their work on time and left early.

NOTE: [This means that only the students drinking strong coffee left early].

EX: The students, drinking strong coffee, finished their work on time and left early.

NOTE: [This means that all of the students were drinking strong coffee and left early].

Parenthetical expressions or phrases may be emphasised more forcefully by using dashes instead of commas.

EX: The students—drinking strong coffee—finished their work on time and left early.

Parenthetical expressions may be at the beginning or at the end of a sentence, as well as in the middle; they may be moved around in a sentence without changing its meaning, although there may be a change of emphasis.

EX: I will not, however, repeat this class with the same instructor.
EX: However, I will not repeat this class with the same instructor.
EX: I will not repeat this class with the same instructor, however.

The above examples illustrate that a parenthetical expression may consist of a single word (as well as several words). In addition to however, other brief parenthetical expressions include the following: in fact, therefore, for instance, accordingly, moreover, and for example.

Parenthetical expressions may also appear in parentheses instead of enclosed between commas. Placing an expression in parentheses will make it stand out more than setting it off with commas, and will break the flow of information even more. If a parenthetical expression is enclosed in parentheses at the end of a sentence it will often be less disruptive, especially if short. Dashes—em dashes—may also be used to set off parentheticals for the most emphasis. This is a matter of choice for the student, depending on the emphasis desired and the level of disruption that results.

EX: I vacationed in several cities last year, Budapest, Hong Kong and Tokyo, until I ran out of money and came home.

EX: I vacationed in several cities last year (Budapest, Hong Kong and Tokyo) until I ran out of money and came home.

It does not matter which you use in some cases, where the flow of information is not interrupted.

EX: I have only two subjects this term, English and maths.
EX: I have only two subjects this term (English and maths).

In other situations, either use may greatly interrupt the flow of information.

EX: I vacationed in several cities last year, after finishing my final exams, before I ran out of money and came home.

EX: I vacationed in several cities last year (after finishing my final exams) before I ran out of money and came home.

PUNCTUATION MARKS

Punctuation problems: missing, not required, or incorrect choice. Punctuation marks are as follows, set in brackets, which are not part of the punctuation marks:

[']   Apostrophe
[,]   Comma
[;]   Semicolon
[:]   Colon
[.]   Full stop or period
[!]   Exclamation point
[?]   Question mark
[' ']   Quotation marks - UK; [" "] - US

Used less often are the hyphen, n-dash, and m-dash, as well as parentheses and square brackets.

You know what you wrote, or at least what you intended to say, but does the reader? The purpose of punctuation is to make it easier for the reader to read and understand your sentences. Some students avoid commas like the plague, while others cannot use enough of them. Overuse will draw the reader's attention to the punctuation marks and away from the content.

Punctuation can change the meaning of sentences.

EX: You are failing the class. [statement]
EX: You are failing the class? [question]

EX: He said I've always been a slacker. [The speaker is a slacker.]
EX: He said, 'I've always been a slacker'. [A third party is the slacker.]

There are strict rules for using commas in certain instances, such as separating two independent clauses—which could each stand alone as a separate sentence, setting apart introductory words or clauses, and enclosing parenthetical expressions in the middle of a sentence between a pair of commas. Only one comma is required if a parenthetical expression starts or ends a sentence.

There are other mandatory rules for the use of commas but you now know the most important ones. Here are a few examples to get you started, although there are more are under COMMAS below.

EX: I went to university for four years, after which I graduated with honours.

EX: However, it required a lot of extra work to succeed.

EX: The school I attended, which was located outside London, was expensive.

In other cases the use of commas is left to the discretion of the writer. Commas should be used wherever you believe it will avoid confusion, uncertainty, or add clarity; otherwise, use them sparingly. You may also use commas to make reading a sentence smoother, even though there would be no confusion without them.

EX: The last bus for school if I want to be on time leaves at nine-thirty every morning.
EX: The last bus for school, if I want to be on time, leaves at nine-thirty every morning. [smoother reading]

COMMAS

The use of commas is not as straightforward as it is for full stops. A few examples are set forth below to illustrate some, but not all, of the uses of commas.

First: to make it clear where a clauses ends, for easier reading and to avoid confusion. If a comma is missing, the reader may not comprehend the correct meaning of what you are saying until reaching the end of the sentence.

INCORRECT: Before leaving the students in the classroom packed up their notebooks.

NOTE: [The sentence starts to lead you to believe that someone is leaving the students, not that the students are leaving.]

CORRECTED: Before leaving, the students in the classroom packed up their notebooks.

NOTE: [In the second example, it is clear that the students are the ones who are leaving; no one is leaving them.]

Second: In cases where the use of a comma is not mandatory, it is a matter of discretion, and a comma may be inserted here and there in order to be helpful to the reader.

For example, if *and* is used between two independent (separate) clauses, a comma will usually be placed before *and*, unless the clauses are short, but there are exceptions so you will have to use your judgment.

EX: Many students have come to the United Kingdom to study, and a large number of them go to universities outside London.

EX: The students usually arrive on time and the instructor usually arrives late.

In any event, you should try to minimize the use of commas in order to improve the flow of information and keep your writing crisp. Remember that you are writing, not speaking. Although you might pause briefly in the middle of a sentence if speaking, the same sentence would not necessarily require a comma if written (though it would not be incorrect to use a comma).

EX (spoken): After paying my tuition, I will be lucky if I have enough money for a cup of tea.

EX (written): After paying my tuition I will be lucky if I have enough money for a cup of tea.

If you have too many commas in a sentence, you should break it up into two or more shorter sentences, or possibly change some of the commas to semicolons.

Third: Commas may be used to make sentences less repetitive, and crisper, by using a comma in place of deleted words.

EX: Juliette wanted to see *Miss You Already* and Thomas wanted to see *Jurassic World*.

EX: Juliette wanted to see *Miss You Already*, and Thomas, *Jurassic World*.

Fourth: Commas are used for series of words or phrases, subject to exceptions, which we will skip. US usage requires the use of the Oxford (or serial) comma – a comma before the 'and' which precedes the last item in the list. UK usage only recommends the final (Oxford) comma if necessary to avoid ambiguity, unless you are required by university rules to follow the Oxford style.

EX (US): Classes offered this term are scriptwriting, directing, and lighting.

EX (UK): Classes offered this term are scriptwriting, directing and lighting.

INCORRECT: I was offered classes in English, and geology.
NOTE: [You need three or more items before commas may be used.]

CORRECTED: I was offered classes in English and geology.

EX: My classes this term are scriptwriting and directing and lighting.

NOTE: [The three items are each connected by a conjunction—and—so no commas are required.]

Fifth: Commas should be used to set off parenthetical expressions or phrases that interrupt a sentence. A parenthetical expression is merely a word or string of words that contains relevant, but non-essential information—something the reader does not need to know in order to understand the thought expressed in the sentence. The use of commas in parenthetical expressions is also discussed above under PARENTHETICAL EXPRESSIONS.

Sixth: Commas are used after introductory clauses unless they are quite short, subject to an exception for certain introductory words, mentioned after the following examples.

EX: Of course I will come to your graduation.
EX: When he arrived at Heathrow for the flight to New York, he realised that he had forgotten his passport.

However, certain introductory words that start a sentence must be followed by a comma: *well*, *yes*, and *in addition*.

EX: Well, I cannot agree with you more.
EX: Yes, what you say is true.
EX: In addition, you should bring a sweater in case the weather turns cold.

When *however* is used to start a sentence as a parenthetical expression it is followed by a comma. If *however* is used to start a sentence with the intended meaning of 'no matter how' or 'in whatever manner', for example, a comma is not used.

EX: However, I will have another slice of apple pie.
EX: However much you like ice cream too many helpings will make you sick.
EX: However did you manage to pass the exam without attending the lectures?

Seventh: Commas are used with multiple adjectives that modify the same noun in cases where each adjective could independently modify the noun.

EX: The amateur rock concert was a loud, tedious experience.

NOTE: The comma is appropriate as either adjective could be used independently.

(1) The amateur rock concert was a loud experience.
(2) The amateur rock concert was a tedious experience.

EX: She bought a bright yellow sports car. [correct]
EX: She bought a bright, yellow sports car. [incorrect]

NOTE: You could say that 'She bought a yellow sports car', but not that 'She bought a bright sports car.' The colour is bright yellow. Therefore, the sentence should not include a comma because the adjectives cannot be used independently.

There are several other uses for commas. Only a few will be illustrated, but without an explanation of the applicable grammar rules. Students frequently omit a comma before which, and go on their merry way. If which is part of a parenthetical expression it must be preceded by a comma. Parenthetical expressions in the middle of a sentence must be enclosed between commas.

EX: One of my goals is to produce a short film by the end of this term, which will be impossible if I don't have enough money to fix my camera in time.

NOTE: [In this example, you could delete the phrase after *term* without changing the meaning of the sentence; the phrase provides additional information but it is not necessary. Thus the use of a comma before *which* is required in the example.]

EX: One of my goals is to produce a short film *that* runs no longer than five-minutes. [non-academic]
EX: One of my goals is to produce a short film which runs no longer than five-minutes. [academic]

NOTE: [If you delete the words in the first example after *film* the meaning of the sentence will change, so that a comma should not be used before *that*. *Which* should be used instead of *that* for academic writing; in the second example, a comma is not required before *which* because there is no parenthetical expression following *film*.]

27

EX: My first film, which should run under twenty minutes, will be completed next week.

NOTE: [The use of commas is correct because deleting the parenthetical phrase would not change the meaning of the sentence.]

The following examples may be written with either *which* or *that*, but *which* is preferred for academic writing and should be used unless it changes the meaning of the sentence.

EX: Any class which lasts more than two hours puts me to sleep. [academic]
EX: Any class that lasts more than two hours puts me to sleep. [non-academic]

NOTE: [A comma is not required before *which* in the above example because the sentence contains no parenthetical phrase or expression.]

Another instance where students often omit required commas is when they use *including* or *which includes* in a sentence, which may or may not involve a list of items.

EX: I have travelled to many places, including Budapest, New York and Hong Kong.
EX: Last summer I travelled all around Europe, including Budapest.
EX: Next term I will take many new subjects, which include acting and directing.

SEMICOLONS

Many students make frequent use of semicolons where a comma is the correct choice, or where a full stop should be used to end a sentence. This often leads to run-on sentences. On the other hand, it seems that a great number of students have never heard of the semicolon, which has never appeared in their work; they rely instead (incorrectly) on overuse of the comma. If semicolons are making your life difficult, you may blame Aldus Manutius, who is said to have invented the semicolon (among other things). Contacting him may be rather difficult as he died some time ago—in 1515. However, if you have a stubborn personality and wish to contact Aldus you can probably find someone online who will offer such services (for a fee, which will no doubt grow by the session) by using a Ouija board or some other occult method. Hopefully you are not so inclined, but if you are gullible enough please remember to pay your tuition for next term before contacting a medium.

Semicolons are used where two independent clauses—meaning clauses that could each stand on their own as separate sentences—are joined together as a single sentence, but are not joined with a conjunction (i.e., *and, but, for, or, nor, so, yet*). The first word after a semicolon does not start a new sentence and is not capitalised unless the word itself is required to be capitalised, e.g., the name of a person.

CORRECT: I passed my driving test the third time; I will not have to take it again.

INCORRECT: I passed my driving test the third time; and I will not have to take it again.

CORRECT: I passed my driving test the third time, and I will not have to take it again.

The most common use is to link two related sentences, especially where one of them is extremely short. A semicolon may also link a sentence in contrast with another sentence that precedes it.

EX: I used to take the bus; now I drive to work.
EX: For many years I drank coffee in the afternoon; now I prefer iced tea.

If you join two clauses with such words as *accordingly, however* or *therefore*, for example, you must use one or two commas in addition to the semicolon, as shown in the following examples.

EX: I fell asleep on the train; *accordingly*, I missed my first class on Monday.
EX: I was late for the mid-term; the instructor, *however*, gave me fifteen minutes extra.
EX: I ordered a large plate of bangers and mash but they were out; *therefore*, I just had a sandwich.

29

We have previously indicated that the same sentence may be written several different ways, which will add variety to your work. Semicolons may also be used for the purpose of variety.

EX: I drink coffee every morning. It helps me stay awake during class.
EX: I drink coffee every morning, and it helps me stay awake during class.
EX: I drink coffee every morning; it helps me stay awake during class.

COMMAS vs SEMICOLONS

Another problem that students often have is mixing up commas and semicolons, using the wrong one. Less often is where a comma should be used instead of a full stop, which frequently involves a sentence fragment that should be joined as part of the preceding sentence.

INCORRECT: The exam lasted all morning. And the hardest part was the last hour.
CORRECT: The exam lasted all morning, and the hardest part was the last hour.
CORRECT: The exam lasted all morning and the hardest part was the last hour.
CORRECT: The exam lasted all morning; the hardest part was the last hour.

You may remember that commas are used to separate words in a list or series of three or more items, with the Oxford comma usually omitted for UK usage.

EX: On my vacation I will visit London, Brighton and Hastings. [UK]
EX: On my vacation I will visit London, Brighton, and Hastings. [US]

Semicolons should separate items in a series when the items have internal punctuation (e.g., commas).

EX: Vacation plans this year include London, England; Budapest, Hungary; and Tokyo, Japan.

EX: Goals to improve my skills this term are as follows: take a computer class, four weeks; learn Final Cut Pro, two weeks; and produce a short video, six weeks.

COLONS

Colons are used to introduce information, often in the form of a list, but not all lists require a colon.

INCORRECT: Some foods to be avoided by those watching their weight are: bangers and mash, fish and chips, and beer.

CORRECT: Some foods to be avoided by those watching their weight are as follows: bangers and mash, fish and chips, and beer. [US]

CORRECT: Some foods to be avoided by those watching their weight are as follows: bangers and mash, fish and chips, and beer. [UK]

NOTE: [Omitting the Oxford comma after chips (generally permitted for UK, not US, usage) should not be done because it would cause confusion as fish and chips is really one item.]

A colon may also be used to provide an explanation or more information about what you have just written.

EX: The instructor said my work had too many mistakes: incorrect punctuation, faulty grammar and too many run-on sentences.

There are several other uses for colons, including placing a colon in front of a short quotation in the case of academic work. Longer quotations may require that you use a block style for the quotation—indented with no quotation marks.

Colons are used to indicate the time in the US, whereas a full stop is used in the UK.

EX: The train is scheduled to leave at 9:45. [US]
EX: The train is scheduled to leave at 9.45. [UK]

APOSTROPHES

Apostrophes—where the bloody hell do they go?

They are used for different purposes, and students often put them in the wrong place, omit them or use them when they should not. Apostrophes are mostly used for possession or contractions, although there are other uses. Reminder: contractions should not find their way into academic writing unless included in a quotation. Some correct and incorrect uses follow.

Ownership or possession:

> EX: My roommate's clothes are all over the place. [one roommate]
> EX: My classmates' compositions are better than mine. [more than one classmate]
> EX: A good night's sleep is recommended before exams.

Possession can also be shown without the use of a contraction; however, some wording is long-winded and not recommended.

> EX: The umbrella belonging to Ashley was stolen yesterday. [long-winded]

> EX: Ashley's umbrella was stolen yesterday. [better]

> EX: Ashley was looking for her umbrella yesterday. [indicates possession]

Possession can also be indicated by using *of* as a possessive with a noun; its use is usually restricted to referring to inanimate objects.

> EX: The left arm of the chair is broken. [correct]
> EX: The left arm of Matthew is broken. [incorrect]
> EX: Matthew's left arm is broken. [correct]

The use of apostrophes can be a bit more complicated when possession refers to more than one person. In the case of joint or shared ownership only the last name has an apostrophe; if ownership is separate each name has an apostrophe.

EX: Rebecca and Gabriella's flat is near the university. [shared]
EX: John's, Anna's and Nicole's iPads went missing yesterday. [separate ownership]

Avoid incorrect use of apostrophes for possession:

INCORRECT: *It's* owner is the woman across the road. [It's means it is, not possession.]
CORRECT: *Its* owner is the woman across the road. [Its indicates possession.]

INCORRECT: Who's automobile is that? [Who's means who is, not possession.]
CORRECT: Whose automobile is that? [Whose indicates possession.]
CORRECT: Who's missing from class today? [Who's means who is.]

Pronouns used <u>without</u> apostrophes, because they already denote possession, include *his, hers, its, ours, yours,* etc.

EX: The red purse is her's. [incorrect]
EX: The red purse is hers. [correct]

Other examples of student difficulties:

INCORRECT: I expect many people to buy DVD's of my film.
CORRECT: I expect many people to buy DVDs of my film.

INCORRECT: The audience conduct at the premiere was quite unexpected.
CORRECT: The audience's conduct at the premiere was quite unexpected.

<u>Contractions:</u>

NON-ACADEMIC USE: I didn't like the grade I received in English.

ACADEMIC USE: I did not like the grade I received in English.

ACADEMIC QUOTE: 'I didn't like the grade I got in English', he said.

NOTE: [Except for showing possession, contractions should not be used in academic or formal work unless included in a quotation that reflects *exactly* what the speaker said.]

Time:

    EX: In three days' time I will be in the Bahamas.
    EX: In three days I will be in the Bahamas.
    EX: After the accident, I received eight weeks' sick pay.
    EX: This bread must be two weeks old.

Location and places:

Apostrophes can also be used to indicate the location of a place in relation to a person.

    EX: My uncle's home is in St. Petersburg.
    EX: The stock broker's office is in the City of London on Cheapside.

QUESTION MARKS

There are three basic types of questions: direct, indirect, and rhetorical. Direct questions require a question mark at the end of a sentence instead of a full stop as do rhetorical questions, which are questions that do not require an answer.

    EX: What time does the movie start? [direct]
    EX: How much longer must we wait to have new elections in this country? [rhetorical]
    EX: I wonder if her grade is better than mine. [indirect]

    NOTE: [An indirect question is really a statement, not a question.]

FULL STOPS (PERIODS)

Full stops, also called periods, are rather simple and should be placed at the end of a sentence, followed by a space. Typing mistakes sometimes happen and failure to proofread carefully has left a space between the last word of a sentence and the full stop in the work of many a student.

EX: My interview went well . I expect a job offer in two weeks. [Do you see the space before the full stop? Looks sloppy, doesn't it?]

NOTE: [This type of error is easier to spot proofreading from a hard copy, unless your software program underlines the problem, and even then, you may miss it.]

NOTE: [The two short sentences above could also be written with a semicolon between.]

EX: My interview went well; I expect a job offer in two weeks.

IT, an abbreviation for information technology, is often incorrectly typed by students as *I.T,* some of whom unfortunately switch back and forth between *I.T* and *IT*.

CAPITALISATION

We'll start with an easy one. The first word of each sentence must always be capitalised. Occasionally one will see words in the middle of a sentence capitalised which should not be, normally the result of carelessness or failure to proofread. A proper name in the middle of a sentence, such as London, would of course be capitalised.

Other mistakes often made by students are capitalising the first letter (or all letters) of a word in the middle of a sentence for emphasis.

EX: I am Always on time for class. [incorrect]
EX: I am *always* on time for class. [correct]
EX: I am NEVER late for class. [incorrect]
EX: I am never late for class. [correct]

The intended purpose of the mid-sentence capitalisation in the last two examples is to add emphasis, which is not only incorrect but often found in students' essays. Instead, emphasis should be achieved by underlining the word in question or placing it in

35

italics. Full capitalization or boldface is not recommended for academic writing. See further discussion below under EMPHASIS.

You must capitalise the names of persons (e.g., Agatha Christie), places (e.g., London) and organizations (e.g., the British Museum), as well as acronyms, such as everyone's favourites—the NHS and HMRC. Except for well-known acronyms (e.g., BBC), spell out the full name the first time it is used followed by the acronym in brackets; then just use the acronym by itself.

The name of a person is always capitalised, no matter where it appears in a sentence. If a full name is used, each name must be capitalised. Some students, more often those whose first language is not English, tend to capitalise only the first name, even where the full name is used in a sentence.

> EX: John *smith* is a very common name. [incorrect]
> EX: John *Smith* is a very common name. [correct]

When a pronoun is used in place of a name, it should only be capitalised if it begins a sentence.

> EX: *She* always arrives on time for class. [correct]
> EX: It is the first time that *She* has missed class. [incorrect]

Titles (e.g., captain) are not capitalised in the middle of a sentence unless used with a person's name.

> INCORRECT: The Captain was late.
> CORRECT: The pilot, Captain Peters, was late.

Students often capitalise words in the middle of a sentence that may appear to be titles, but are really job descriptions, such as Director, Producer, Screenwriter, etc. These should not be capitalised, even if used in connection with a person's name, unless they begin a sentence.

> EX: The Director of *The Birds* was Alfred Hitchcock. [incorrect]
> EX: The director of *The Birds* was Alfred Hitchcock. [correct]

EX: British Director Carol Reed is best known for *The Third Man*. [incorrect]
EX: British director Carol Reed is best known for *The Third Man*. [correct]

EX: Italian Director Federico Fellini won the Palme d'Or for *La Dolce Vida*. [incorrect]
EX: Director Federico Fellini won the Palme d'Or for *La Dolce Vida*. [correct]

The titles of works must also be capitalised, including the following: books, plays, motion pictures and TV programs. Brand names of products must also be capitalised (without including ™), such as Skype and Twitter, which students frequently fail to capitalise. Another fault of students is capitalising the word *Festival* when writing about film festivals; it should only be capitalised when used as part of the name of a specific festival. The same is true of *law*, which should only be capitalised if used as part of the name of a particular law or statute.

Students have been known to capitalise only the first word of a book or movie title, or in the case of a product the entire name is in lowercase. Note that articles, such as *a*, *in* or *the*, for example, are not capitalised in the middle of titles.

EX: Murder on the orient express   [incorrect]
EX: Murder on the Orient Express   [correct]

EX: The man in the white suit   [incorrect]
EX: *The Man in the White Suit*   [correct]

EX: Farewell, my lovely   [incorrect]
EX: *Farewell, My Lovely*   [correct]

EX: final cut pro   [incorrect]
EX: Final Cut Pro   [correct]

EX: Adobe premiere   [incorrect]
EX: Adobe Premiere   [correct]

Do not capitalise *the* in the middle of a sentence unless it is part of the name or title. There is no rule that will yield the correct result each time; you will have to look up titles and names.

EX: We may visit *the* National Gallery next week.
EX: I read about *The* Bank of England in *The Economist*.

Capitalisation should also be used for days (e.g., Monday), documents (e.g., Magna Carta), cities (e.g., Brighton), places (e.g., Trafalgar Square), holidays (e.g., Boxing Day), historical events (e.g., the Battle of Waterloo), institutions (e.g., the Royal Academy of Art), buildings (e.g., the Shard), government bodies (e.g., HMRC), personal and business names and a long list of others. Full stops are not placed between the letters of acronyms (e.g., HMRC, UK).

CAPITALISATION AND PUNCTUATION – LISTS AND HEADINGS

Vertical and horizontal lists are somewhat different in punctuation and style. Vertical lists will be discussed first as they are more varied. A list may be placed in the body of your work or in a template included as part of the work. In either case, for items listed vertically do not capitalise the first word of each item and do not put a full stop at the end of any of them (including the last item), unless the items constitute complete sentences. If so, capitalise the first word of each item and end each with a full stop. Listed items with internal punctuation (e.g., a comma) should be followed by a semicolon, the last one with a full stop. Numbers or letters may be used to list items in their order of importance; bullet points may also be used where items are not listed in order of sequence or importance. Another alternative is to use the word *to* (instead of numbers, letters or bullet points) in order to introduce each item.

Whether or not information that introduces a list requires a colon depends on the form of the introductory phrase. A colon should follow introductory words that introduce a list only if the introductory words could stand alone as a sentence and end with a full stop; this rule applies whether the items in the list are words, phrases or full sentences themselves. No punctuation should be used if the list is introduced by an incomplete sentence. In no event should a semicolon be used to start a vertical list.

EX: Even the essays of graduate-level students often contain spelling, grammar and other mistakes:

- excessive use of commas
- inconsistent spelling of the same words
- improper capitalisation
- run-on-sentences
- sentence fragments

EX: The university now offers courses such as

- film history
- screenplay writing
- directing
- editing

EX: My favourite classes are

(a) acting
(b) directing
(c) screenplay writing

In addition to numbers, letters and bullet points, the word *to* may also be used to introduce each item in a list.

EX: My goals this term are

to attend all classes
to take better notes
to complete all assignments on time

Vertical lists generally do not contain internal punctuation. However, semicolons are used when the items in a list contain internal punctuation.

EX: Top tourist locations include

- London, England;
- Paris, France; and
- New York, New York.

Items in vertical lists (as well as those in horizontal lists) must be parallel in expression and format.

EX: He likes to eat Chinese food, hockey and going to the cinema. [incorrect]

EX: He likes Chinese food, hockey and the cinema. [correct]
EX: He likes eating Chinese food, playing hockey and going to the cinema. [correct]
EX: He likes to eat Chinese food, play hockey and to go to the cinema. [incorrect]
EX: He likes to eat Chinese food, play hockey and go to the cinema. [correct]

INCORRECT	CORRECT
Career goals	Career goals
become an actor	to be an actor
to be a director	to be a director
writing screenplays	to be a screenplay writer

Following is a general discussion of horizontal lists, together with examples. Horizontal lists are often sentences, usually short ones.

EX: International travel requires a suitcase, ticket and passport.
EX: Travel requires several items such as time, money and a suitcase.
EX: Travel requires several items; time, money and a suitcase are necessary.
EX: I need to buy the following: shoes, socks, shirts and a hat.
EX: I have taken several classes this term: music, maths, grammar and business.
EX: We have been to London, England; St. Petersburg, Russia; and Tokyo, Japan.
EX: We visited several countries: China, Japan and Singapore.

Horizontal lists may be numbered or unnumbered.

EX: I have lived in several cities: (1) London, (2) Paris and (3) Hong Kong. [UK]
EX: I have lived in several cities: London, Paris, and Hong Kong. [US]

A colon is used after a complete sentence that introduces a list or if the sentence includes (1) the following, (2) as follows, (3) will include, etc.

EX: Classes this term will include: acting, directing and editing.

EX: Specials today are as follows: bacon butty, fish 'n' chips, broiled haddock.

Some students incorrectly use a semicolon to start a list. A semicolon may only be used, instead of a colon, for a horizontal list if the introductory sentence is followed by a transitional word or phrase.

EX: Many foods are not healthy; for example, hot dogs, beer and French fries.

Full stops should not be used after chapters, titles, headings or subheadings.

INCORRECT	CORRECT
LIST OF GOALS THIS TERM.	LIST OF GOALS THIS TERM
1. Attend every class,	1. Attend every class
2. Avoid arriving late for classes;	2. Avoid arriving late for classes
3. Staying awake during lecturers.	3. Stay awake during lecturers

NOTE: In addition to correcting punctuation in the list, the wording in item 3 is changed in order to comply with the parallel construction rule.

QUOTATION MARKS

How to properly use quotations and references in academic work is not a topic covered in detail in this book. Quotation marks may be used for emphasis as previously noted. However, they are more often used to state what a person said or wrote, in the exact word order. Quotation marks may not be used if the word order or any word is changed. Indirect quotations should not be in quotation marks, even though the meaning is the same.

       EX (direct):   The instructor said, 'Hand in all work by Friday'. [British]
       EX (direct):   The instructor said, "Hand in all work by Friday." [American]
       EX (indirect): The instructor said to hand in all work by Friday. [indirect]

       NOTE: [Punctuation (e.g., full stop or question mark) goes outside the closing quotation mark for British usage, inside for American.]

The first word of a quotation must be capitalised.

       EX (incorrect): The conductor said, 'have your tickets ready'.
       EX (correct):   The conductor said, 'Have your tickets ready'.

Quotations within quotations are not that difficult. If you use single quotation marks for the outside quote (British), use double quotation marks for the inside quote.

       EX (UK):   John said, 'Winston Churchill had the right idea about conservation of energy: "Never stand up when you can sit down, and never sit down when you can lie down"'.

If you use double quotation marks for the outside quote (American), use single quotation marks for the inside quote.

       EX (US):   John said, "Winston Churchill had the right idea about conservation of energy: 'Never stand up when you can sit down, and never sit down when you can lie down.'"

Do not even think about putting a quote within a quote within a quote unless you want to confuse the reader. Instead, rewrite so that it will read smoothly.

Block quotations are long quotes (usually four, five or six or more lines, depending on who you ask) which are indented in block form without quotation marks. Quotes within a block quotation will be enclosed with either single (UK) or double (US) quotation marks, as appropriate. Opinion also varies as to whether block quotations should be a different font or type size. You will need to check your university's requirements. Students frequently forget to indent block quotations.

One more thing: You should capitalise the first word of a complete quotation but not a partial quotation.

EX: The professor said that anyone caught cheating on the exam would be 'marched out the door and over to the dean's office'.

CITATIONS AND STATISTICS

Statistics and other specific facts should be supported by citing the source. Do not state opinions as facts. Saying that Hollywood accounting' usually calculates 'net profits' in a way that deprives investors from sharing in the success of a box office hit is one thing. Saying that a film with a worldwide gross of £850,000,000 (as reported in *The Hollywood Reporter*) was profitable is an assumption and not a fact if the net profit numbers are not reported, which they usually are not. If you state the population or number of movie theatres in China, the source should be cited. You may find different numbers from various sources, in which case it is even more important to cite the source you are quoting.

ITALICS

Since we have mentioned books and movie titles, let's discuss *italics*. As you can see italicised words are slanted a bit to the right, sort of like the *Leaning Tower of Pisa*, depending on which side you view it from. Italics may be used for emphasis, or to draw attention to an unusual word or an unfamiliar foreign word, but are more often used for titles of certain works, which should also be capitalised, including books, plays, operas, paintings, motion pictures, and TV programs, among others. Magazines and newspapers are italicised, but articles from them are placed in quotation marks, as are episodes of TV programs. An album title should be in italics, but individual song titles should be in quotation marks.

INCORRECT	CORRECT
EX: <u>The King's Speech</u>	*The King's Speech*
EX: 'The Ladykillers'	*The Ladykillers*
EX: Murder On The Orient *Express*	*Murder on the Orient* Express

NOTE: ['On' and 'the' in the last example should be italicised, but not capitalized.]

EMPHASIS

Students sometimes use boldface or fully capitalised words in the middle of a sentence for emphasis, but neither should be used in academic work. Instead, emphasis can be achieved by <u>underlining</u> the word in question or placing it in *italics;* never do both. The use of quotation marks for emphasis should be used sparingly, and preferably not in academic writing. If you use italics or underlining for emphasis in your work, be consistent and use one or the other, not both. Emphasis should be shown in academic writing by the use and arrangement of words and phrases, rather than using underlining, italics, or boldface. You can change word order for emphasis; try moving words around and rearranging your sentence until the desired result is achieved.

EX: Maths, to my great surprise, was the worst class I ever took.
EX: The worst class I ever took, to my great surprise, was maths.

You can also use emphasis by inserting an extremely short sentence after a long one.
EX: I am sick and tired of you constantly criticising my English. Drop Dead!

If you repeat what you are saying for emphasis, instead of underlining or using italics, the result will most likely be redundancy.

EX: I got the lowest grade in the class, and could not have done worse.
EX: I received the *lowest* grade in the class.

Certain words, such as *however*, may also be used for emphasis but their overuse will lose their effectiveness and disrupt smooth reading of your work. Although *however* may be used for emphasis, it is primarily used for contrast. *However* may start a sentence or may join two simple sentences to form a compound sentence; in the latter case the clause after *however* either minimizes the preceding clause or is in contrast with it.

EX: Concert tickets are expensive; however, they can be purchased at a discount.

Parenthetical expressions may also be set off with dashes—em dashes—for emphasis.

EX: I'll tell you when I will return to that café—never.

EX: The price of that fancy car—£130,000—is ridiculous.

SEPARATE OR COMBINED WORDS

Student work often reflects the use of two separate words, when they should be combined as one word. To make matters worse, many students are inconsistent throughout their work, alternating correct and incorrect spelling or word combinations, being either indecisive or possibly calculating that this way they will be right fifty percent of the time. This might be appreciated by a bookmaker, but not by the person grading your work. Consistency makes a nicer looking presentation, even if a word is used incorrectly.

Following are several examples found in the work of university-level students.

INCORRECT	CORRECT
Camera man	Cameraman
Class mates	Classmates
Film maker	Filmmaker
Multi task	Multitask
Team mate	Teammate
Script writer	Scriptwriter
Screen play	Screenplay
Work load	Workload

45

Cannot vs can not

The general consensus is that you may use either *cannot* or *can not* in most situations, although *cannot* is preferred, and is recommended for academic writing. Nevertheless, some word processing programs will highlight *can not* as being incorrect. You may think that you can avoid choosing which spelling to use by using can't instead; however, *can't* may not be used for academic writing.

You would not use *cannot* where *not* is used to be emphatic.

EX: You *can not* go to the cinema unless you finish washing the dishes. [*Can not* is correctly used for emphasis instead of *cannot*.]

You may need to rewrite a sentence in order to convert it from speech (or informal writing) to formal writing, but it may require substantial rewording instead of a simple change.

EX: You may say, 'Why can't I win the lottery at least once?' [speech]

NOTE: You may not change the sentence to a formal style by writing 'Why cannot I win the lottery at least once?' [Rewording is required.]

EITHER COMBINED OR SEPARATE WORDS MAY BE CORRECT, DEPENDING ON USAGE

The following words have different meanings and should be chosen with care by students. Although the context of your sentence may make the intended meaning clear, your grade will slip a bit in the mind of your instructor by using the wrong choice.

Any one   EX: *Any one* of these topics is acceptable for your term paper.
Anyone   EX: *Anyone* who arrives late will not be admitted to take the exam.

Every day   EX: *Every day* I get up early to be on time for class.

Everyday   EX: *Everyday* prices are getting more
expensive each year.

Every one   EX: *Every one* of you has passed this term.
Everyone   EX: *Everyone* is to be here at noon on
Friday.

In to   EX: I was hoping to get *in to* deposit my
check before the bank closes.
Into   EX: She went *into* the professor's office ten
minutes ago.

May be   EX: It *may be* that you will fail the class
again this term.
Maybe   EX: *Maybe* you will follow the instructions
more carefully next time.

On to   EX: Even though it was very late, she drove
on to Reading.
Onto   EX: He stepped *onto* the pavement and
slipped on the ice.

Over time   EX: *Over time* I have learnt to be patient.
Overtime   EX: I am tired of working *overtime* at my job.

Set up   EX: I need to *set up* the camera before the
director arrives.
Setup   EX: The *setup* is very nice, but the ticket
booth should be on the left.

Some time   EX: Perhaps we can find *some time* to go to
London this next week.
Sometime   EX: I will call you *sometime* next week.

Whereas EX: I prefer noir, *whereas* she prefers comedies.
[correct]
Where as EX: I prefer noir, *where as* she prefers comedies.
[incorrect]

NOTE: In the above examples *whereas* is used for
comparison. In a different context *where as* may be used,
as in the following example:

47

EX: She joined the Treasury, where as Chancellor of the Exchequer she was highly respected. [In this example *where as* has an entirely different meaning from *whereas*; such use is generally quite limited.]

HYPHENS

Hyphens serve many purposes, which we will illustrate with several examples. By the way, although we believe that our book is less tedious than the average grammar book—though this is technically not a grammar book—we assume that you have the good sense to have a strong cup of coffee nearby as you continue reading. Prefixes sometimes require hyphens, and sometimes not, as discussed in the next section.

Some correct and incorrect examples:

INCORRECT	CORRECT
Above average	Above-average
Seven minute film	Seven-minute film

Other correct examples:

Day-to-day
Time-to-time
Year-on-year
Six-year-old automobile
One hundred and seventy-five thousand [British]
One hundred seventy-five thousand [American]

Hyphens should not be used between *adverbs* ending in -*ly* and the words that follow them.

a recently-released movie   [incorrect]
a recently released movie   [correct]

a highly-recommended restaurant   [incorrect]
a highly recommended restaurant   [correct]

However, a hyphen is used where the –*ly* word is *not* an adverb.

EX: Beware of that friendly-looking used car salesperson.

EX: They recommended a family-owned bed and breakfast in Eastbourne.

Eliminate ambiguity (of word meaning) with hyphens when necessary.

EX: You should recover the patio furniture if the police do their job. [get back]
EX: You should re-cover the patio furniture. [cover up again]

EX: The professor is also a short story writer. [ambiguous]
EX: The professor is also a short-story writer. [the stories are short]

NOTE: Is the professor a short person who writes stories, or a writer of short stories?

Compound numbers that are spelt out (from twenty-one through ninety-nine) require hyphens.

EX: Twenty-one is my favourite number.
EX: One hundred seventy-five pounds is the most I will pay.

Hyphens between two words can change the meaning of a sentence or phrase.

EX: four-year-old bottles of wine [indeterminate number of bottles that are each four years old]
EX: four year-old bottles of wine [four bottles that are one year old]

EX: The instructor made an unkind remark about my essay. [comment]
EX: I asked the instructor to re-mark my essay in hopes of a better grade. [mark again]

EX: They have a little used automobile. [small-sized]
EX: They have a little-used automobile. [infrequent]

Now for the tricky part; whether a hyphen is required sometimes depends on word order.

EX: He is well-known as a slacker.
EX: His reputation as a slacker is well known.

EX: Her lectures are first class.

EX: He only completed one-half of the assignment.
EX: One-half of the students completed their assignments.

EX: She has a part-time job.
EX: She works part time.

EX: He is a well-established musician.
EX: He is well established in the music industry.

EX: She is a well-known actress.
EX: She is well known for her sense of humour.

PREFIXES

Prefixes sometimes require hyphens, and sometimes not. This is often the result of differing opinions of various dictionaries and differences between British and American usage. When in doubt, look it up.

INCORRECT	CORRECT
e-mail	email
non fiction	non-fiction
non sense	nonsense
pre-historic	prehistoric
preindustrial	pre-industrial
sub-plot	subplot
un aware	unaware

When the last letter of a prefix is the same as the first letter of the word following it a hyphen must be used.

INCORRECT	CORRECT
antiinflationary	anti-inflationary
nonnegotiable	non-negotiable
reenter	re-enter

50

NUMBERS

Numbers from one to ten should be spelt out. UK usage allows the writer to choose whether to write round numbers as words or figures. However, numbers that start a sentence should be spelt out.

EX: 10 students will receive scholarships this year. [incorrect]

EX: Ten students will receive scholarships this year. [correct]

Where there are two consecutive numbers in a sentence, spelling out one of the numbers may be required in order to avoid confusion.

EX: In 2015 16 students graduated. [confusing]

EX: In 2015, sixteen students graduated. [clear]

The following examples show how dates should be written for UK and US usage.

EX: All essays must be turned in no later than 11 January. [UK]

EX: All essays must be turned in no later than January 11th. [US]

WORDS EXISTING IN SINGULAR FORM ONLY

INCORRECT	CORRECT
Equipments	Equipment
Feedbacks	Feedback
Softwares	Software

Examples:

INCORRECT: I have used many equipment's during this term.
CORRECT: I used much equipment this term.

NON-ACADEMIC: This equipment's broken.
ACADEMIC: This equipment is broken.

Remember: contractions should not be used in academic work, except to show possession or in quotations.

INCORRECT: I bought many equipments' for my class project.
CORRECT: I bought many pieces of equipment for my class project.

INCORRECT: I have been using many softwares' during the year.
CORRECT: The software's life was shorter than advertised.

Some uncountable nouns ending in 's' exist only in singular form (although they look plural):

Athletics
Economics
Gymnastics
Linguistics
Maths or Mathematics
News
Physics
Statistics

There are two things to remember about uncountable nouns that end in 's': (1) do not use *a* or *an* before them; and (2) use a singular verb with them.

EX: Mathematics *are* not easy for many students. [incorrect]
EX: Mathematics *is* not easy for many students. [correct]

EX: Last term I took a economics. [incorrect: economics is a noun]
EX: Last term I took economics. [correct]
EX: Last term I took an economics class. [correct: economics is used as an adjective]

Words (uncountable nouns) which can be used only in the plural form require a plural verb, and must not be used with *a* or *an*:

Ashes
Clothes
Glasses
Headphones
Jeans
Scissors

EX: A glasses was left in the classroom last Friday. [incorrect]
EX: A pair of glasses was left in the classroom last Friday. [correct]

Words that look singular, but are plural:

Cattle
People
Police

Phrases of measurement use a singular verb:

Twenty-five thousand pounds *is* a lot of money for a new car.
Thirty-two kilos *is* the maximum weight allowed for checked luggage on some airlines.

Four kilometres *is* too far to walk, especially in the rain.

COMMONLY CONFUSED WORDS – SAME SOUND

Although commonly confused words that sound the same have different meanings, some have more than one meaning, as shown by the examples listed below.

A lot/alot/allot:

The word *alot* does not exist, although often used in place of *a lot*, which means a great number of things or people. The word lot (referring to land) does exist and *a lot* may be used in a different context (e.g., a parcel of land), as two separate words.

EX: Our new neighbour has a lot of money. [much]

EX: There were a lot of students at the concert last night. [many]

EX: A lot in our area recently sold for a record one million pounds. [vacant land]

EX: I wish my stockbroker would allot me more shares on this offering. [apportion]

EX: You must allot sufficient time to each question to pass the exam. [divide]

Already/all ready:

EX: It is *already* too late to make reservations for New Year's at the Savoy. [time]

EX: We are *all ready* to leave if you are. [each one is prepared]

EX: Is it *already* December? [so soon]

Altogether/all together:

EX: We were *all together* for Christmas and Boxing Day. [a group]

EX: We were *altogether* wrong about what he wanted for his birthday. [entirely]

Anyway/any way/anyways:

EX: Smart phones are expensive, but I'm going to buy one *anyway*. [regardless]

EX: Do you know *any way* to save money on theatre tickets? [means or manner]

EX: The café closed early. Anyways, I am not that hungry. [avoid: very informal]

NOTE: [If you cannot rewrite the sentence using *in any manner* in place of *any way*, use *anyway* instead of *any way*, as in the first example.]

Are/our:

EX: *Are* you ready for the results of the exam? [verb: to be]

EX: *Our* patio has the most beautiful garden in the development. [possession: plural form of my]

<u>Board/bored</u>:

In addition to having different meanings when used as nouns, more possibilities for confusion arise when these words are used as verbs.

EX: I need another *board* to finish my patio. [noun: wood]
EX: The *board* (of directors) presently has nine members. [noun: group]

EX: The students were *bored* long before the lecture was over. [verb: uninterested]

EX: *Board* up the windows before the storm arrives. [verb: cover up]
EX: You should board the express train ten minutes before departure. [verb: get on]

EX: The burglars *bored* a hole through the wall safe in no time at all. [verb: drill]

<u>Brake/break</u>:

EX: I bought a used bicycle but the *brake* does not work properly. [noun: bike part]
EX: If I need to stop suddenly, I cannot *brake* in time to avoid an accident. [verb: stop]

EX: Be careful; if you *break* that vase, it will cost you fifty pounds. [verb: damage]
EX: If you *break* your promise, you will regret it. [verb: not keep]

EX: I asked the policeman to give me a *break* this time. [noun: a reprieve]
EX: Do not expect a *break* in the weather. [noun: change]

<u>Clause/claws</u>:

EX: A *clause* is a group of related words with a noun and a verb. [definition]
EX: I should have read each *clause* of my contract more carefully. [part of document]

EX: The cat decided to exercise its *claws* on my new sofa. [sharp part of an animal]

EX: Each time he falls, he *claws* his way back up the mountain. [climbs]

Complement/compliment:

EX: I will *complement* my education with summer studies in Australia. [supplement]

EX: The instructor gave me a compliment about my essay. [praise]

Dear/deer:

EX: My best friend is very *dear* to me. [much loved]

EX: The price of the necklace is too *dear* for me at this time. [expensive]

EX: *Deer* do not make good household pets. [animals]

EX: Oh dear! I left my umbrella on the bus. [exclamation]

Emigrate/immigrate:

EX: Many railroad workers immigrated to Australia in the 19th century. [came to]

EX: Convicts also emigrated from the United Kingdom, not by choice. [leave]

Fair/fare:

EX: The movie reviews rated the film no better than *fair*. [average]

EX: Some of the students felt that their grades were not *fair*. [treated equally]

EX: The thief was tall, medium build and had *fair* hair. [light colour]

EX: Railway *fares* increase every year. [price of ticket]

EX: The trade *fair* will last three days. [exhibition]

EX: Each weekend offers many arts and crafts fairs. [festival or outdoor market place]

Forward/foreword:

EX: The foreword in the book was written by my professor. [introduction before text of book]
EX: I look *forward* to Friday afternoons, but not Monday mornings. [anticipation]
EX: Please *forward* your essays to the professor no later than this Thursday. [send]
EX: Taking computer classes will *forward* your chances of employment. [advance]
EX: He faced *forward*, listening to the professor's every word. [towards the front]

NOTE: *Towards* is British usage; *toward* is American.

Hole/whole:

EX: The dog keeps getting out through a *hole* in the fence. [gap or opening]
EX: She found herself in a *hole* again. [embarrassing situation]
EX: There is a *hole* in your argument. [flaw]
EX: I can't believe it; he ate the *whole* mince pie. [entire]
EX: She has a *whole* set of Agatha Christie novels. [complete]

Know/no:

EX: Do you *know* how to get to Piccadilly? [knowledge or familiar with]
EX: *No*, I do not want to see that movie again. [negative response]

Maybe/may be:

EX: *Maybe* you will study enough to pass the course this time.
EX: It *may be* that you will not study enough to pass the course.

Past/passed:

EX: Last term I *passed* all of my classes with flying colours. [completed]
EX: We *passed* Buckingham Palace on the way to Hyde Park. [went by]
EX: I fell asleep on the bus and went *past* my stop. [beyond]
EX: In the *past* we lived on a farm. [previous time]
EX: The farthing is a thing of the *past*. [no longer existing]
EX: The *past* president of the university was hit by a lorry last week. [previous]

NOTE: [He was killed by the lorry; that is why he is now the *past* president. It's a joke, in case you are wondering.]

Patience/patients:

INCORRECT: One of my job skills is *patients* with customers.
CORRECT: One of my job skills is *patience* with customers.

EX: *Patients* cannot get same-day appointments with NHS.

Principal/principle:

EX: The school has a new *principal* this year. [head of the school]
EX: The principal reason most students give for arriving late is missing the bus. [primary or main]
EX: My *principles* will not allow me to vote for either candidate. [beliefs]
EX: The *principles* of modern physics are not my favourite topic. [rules]

Red/read:

EX: My new car is red. [colour]
EX: I read an interesting article about investing. [understand written words]
EX: My cousin read law at university. [studied law]

Right/write:

EX: You are always *right*. [correct]
EX: Walk along Piccadilly to Green Park; then turn *right*.
[direction: opposite of left]
EX: Turn round; Hyde Park is *right* there. [location]
EX: You must *write* more than 500 words about your career
choice. [compose]
EX: The constable told the criminal that he had the right to
remain silent. [privilege granted by law to do or refrain from doing
something]

Stationary/stationery:

EX: That constable across the street has been stationary
for one hour. [not moving]
EX: I need to order some stationery for my new business.
[writing paper and envelopes]

To/too/two:

EX: I will go *to* Piccadilly Circus tomorrow. [motion in the
direction of a destination]
EX: Return the book *to* her no later than Friday. [identifying
person affected]

EX: I spent *too* much time on the last exam question.
[excessive]
EX: I like cricket *too*. [also]
EX: It is only *two* more hours. [number]

Their/they're/there:

EX: The red one is *their* automobile. [ownership or
possession]
EX: They're always the last students to leave. [contraction
for they are, which should be used instead of they're for
academic work]
EX: You left your computer over *there*. [place or location]

NOTE: A sentence must have a subject, although there is
an exception, which we will not mention. By now, this

should not surprise you. If a sentence has no subject, then either *there* or *it* must be used as a dummy subject.

EX: *There* is a hole in my new sweater.
EX: *There* is a sale on High Street tomorrow.
EX: *There* is not enough time to eat dinner before the theatre.
EX: Who is *it*?
EX: *It* would be nice to have more holidays.
EX: *It* is time for afternoon tea.

Waive/wave:

EX: A large *wave* caught the surfer off guard and he fell over. [movement of water]
EX: She did not *wave* goodbye before boarding the train. [hand motion]
EX: The landlord would not agree to *waive* the security deposit. [forgo or relinquish]

COMMONLY CONFUSED WORDS – SIMILAR SOUND

Accept/except:

EX: The instructor *accepted* my assignment late because I had the flu. [received]
EX: Everyone *except* me arrived on time. [excluding]

Advice/advise:

EX: I need some investment *advice*. [suggestion]
EX: What would you *advise* me to order? [recommend]

Affect/effect:

EX: My grammar is excellent so I do not think failure to proofread my work will *affect* my grade. [influence]
EX: The *effect* of my poor grades last term has forced me to study harder. [results]

Cite/site/sight:

EX: I forgot to *cite* the source of the quotations in my last term paper. [refer to]
EX: The *site* of the university, two kilometres from my flat, is convenient. [location]
EX: The most beautiful *sight* is a winning lottery ticket in my hand. [visual]

Later/latter:

EX: I am busy now; I will call you back *later*. [subsequent time]
EX: I like white wine and red wine, but I prefer the *latter*. [the last mentioned]

Loose/lose:

EX: The pants are too *loose*; I need a smaller size. [not fitting tight enough]
EX: The race track is a good place to *lose* money. [suffer a loss]

Personal/personnel:

EX: It is a *personal* matter I that do not care to discuss. [private]
EX: The employer cut back of the number of *personnel* they need. [staff]

WRONG WORD CHOICE

Amount/Number:

EX: The *amount* of time I spend studying each week is not enough. [not counted]

EX: The *number* of hits I get on my blog each day is unbelievable. [can be counted]

As if/like:

EX: It looks *as if* I will have to repeat this class. [probability]

EX: She looks *like* the teacher I had two years ago. [similar or resembles]

Between/among:

Between has traditionally been used with reference to two people or items, whereas *among* has been used for three or more, although the usage is changing and some sources state that *between* may now be used for more than two. However, for academic writing you should stick to traditional usage.

EX: Free tickets will be distributed *among* the students present today.

EX: The desert—chocolate layer cake—was divided *between* Harry and Anna.

Can/may:

Can means that you have the ability to do something, not that you should.

EX: You *can* use contractions (e.g., I'm) in academic work, but you should not.

May means permission or possibility to do something.

EX: You *may* see me after class if you wish to discuss your marks. [permission]

EX: I *may* go to Wimbledon next week. [possibility]

These rules also apply when the words are used negatively.

EX: You *cannot* turn in your composition on Monday because the university will be closed for Bank Holiday.

EX: You *may* not use quotations in your work without proper citations.

Farther/Further:

EX: Is Heathrow *farther* from London than Gatwick? [distance]

EX: I cannot walk much *further*; I need to find a taxi. [additional]

EX: I do not want to discuss this any *further*. [refers to time]
EX: I want to *further* my education. [increase]

Fewer/less:

In addition to the uses indicated below in brackets, these words can be differentiated as follows: fewer is used for things that can be counted, less for those that cannot.

EX: There are *fewer* students at university this term. [not as many]

EX: It takes *less* time to get here if I take the express train. [not as much]

Former/latter:

Former and latter are used, in that order, when two things (not more) are referred to in a sentence.

EX: Between the professor and the lecturer, the *former* is a stickler for punctuality.

EX: Between chocolate, strawberry and vanilla, I prefer the *latter*. [incorrect]

From/since:

Both *from* and *since* are used to describe an action from a specific starting point, although *from* may have a stopping point (either in the past or future) or continue indefinitely. *Since* is used to indicate that something started at a specific time in the past and is continuing to the present.

EX: British actor Terry-Thomas lived *from* 10 July 1911 to 8 January 1990.

EX: The cinema will be closed for renovations *from* next Monday.

EX: Julia has not been to London *since* she moved to Ashford.

EX: John has been in England *since* the first of the month.

NOTE: Since can also be used as a synonym for because—to introduce an explanation.

EX: I am going to stay away from the Black Friday sales *since* I have no money.

However, in some cases *since* cannot be substituted for *because* unless the structure of the sentence is changed.

EX: Class was cancelled because of heavy snow. [correct]

EX: Class was cancelled since heavy snow. [incorrect]

EX: Class was cancelled since it snowed heavily. [correct as reworded]

Good/well:

EX: My chances of graduating are good this time. [good is an adjective, modifying chances]

EX: I did *well* on my final exams. [well is an adverb, modifying did]

EX: My chances of graduating are good this time because I did well on my final exams.

NOTE: In some cases, either good or well will work in a sentence, but the meaning will be different.

EX: If I'm good enough I will compete in the marathon next week. [ability]

EX: If I'm well enough I will compete in the marathon next week. [healthy]

Like/as/such as/just as:

EX: The bus does not run on Sundays *like* it used to. [incorrect]

EX: The bus does not run of Sundays *as* it used to. [correct]

EX: I enjoy old movies *like The Third Man.* [incorrect]
EX: I enjoy old movies *such as The Third Man.* [correct]

EX: *Like* I expected, the movie was awful. [incorrect]
EX: *Just as* I expected, the movie was awful. [correct]

There is/there are:

Later in the book we suggest that it is better to reword a sentence than to begin it with *there are*. However, if you choose not to follow this advice it will still be necessary to decide whether to use *there is* or *there are*. The answer can be determined by rewording the sentence in its natural order.

EX: *There are* five students in the front row.

NOTE: [If you reword the sentence (Five students *are* in the front row), it is clear that *there are* should be used; you cannot use 'five students *is*.']

Whether/if:

Whether and *if* can often be substituted without changing the meaning of a sentence.

EX: They wondered whether the cinema had reopened.
EX: They wondered if the cinema had reopened.

The next examples illustrate the use of the words *or not*.

EX: Elizabeth asked *whether* they should go to Bluewater or not. [conversation]
EX: Elizabeth asked *whether or not* they should go to Bluewater. [academic]

Who/that:

EX: The students *who* attend every class will pass the course. [correct]

65

EX: The students *that* attend every class will pass the course. [incorrect]

EX: The cinema *that* I used to go to was torn down last week. [informal]

EX: The cinema *which* I used to go to was torn down last week. [academic]

NOTE: [*Who* refers to persons; *that* refers to your pet turtle and everything else.]

Who/whom:

INCORRECT: *Whom* was the person who telephoned me last night around midnight?

CORRECT: *Who* was the person who telephoned me last night around midnight?

Thinking whether to use *who* or *whom* can result in severe headaches, and possibly loss of hair (according to unconfirmed rumours). Do not get steamed up about it and throw your computer through the window after several moments of indecision; instead, highlight the entire sentence in yellow and come back to it later. Back in the day (which you would not use in academic writing), before work was required to be submitted electronically, you could type either word and cover it up with a coffee stain or cigarette smudge if you were unsure—so much for progress.

Why should you need to know the rules for using *whom* when its everyday use has been dying out for decades? As the American humourist Calvin Trillin said: 'As far as I'm concerned, *whom* is a word that was invented to make everyone sound like a butler'. Unfortunately its proper use is still required in academic writing, so you may encounter a few headaches.

Regrettably we must discuss grammar briefly in order to explain the rules, which basically say that *who* should be used as the subject of a sentence, while *whom* should be used as an object and after a preposition. Another way to decide which word to use is to substitute *he* or *him* in the sentence; if *he* works better, use *who*, and if *him* works better, use *whom*. If the sentence is a question, change the word order to make it a statement instead of a question before you try these substitutions.

EX: *Who* left a navy jacket in the classroom yesterday?

NOTE: [If you change the question into a statement, 'He left a navy jacket in the classroom yesterday', the statement works and you should use *who* instead of *whom*. *Him* does not work as a substitute, so you cannot use *whom*.]

EX: You said she is going to the cinema with *whom*?

NOTE: [If you change the question into a statement, 'You said she is going to the cinema with he', the sentence does not work; you should use *whom* and not *who*.]

EX: The person *who* called did not leave a message.

NOTE: [Here you only use part of the sentence as a test and come up with 'He did not leave a message', so the use of *who* is correct. You cannot say 'him did not leave a message', so you cannot use *whom*.]

Now for a little humour.

EX: The person to whom you are speaking is not here right now. Please call again later.

NOTE: [The person answering the phone does not want to speak to the caller and therefore makes a statement that does not seem to make any sense, though it is grammatically correct.]

WRONG COMBINATIONS

Compare to/compare with:

EX: The weather in Edinburgh *compared to* Glasgow is not any better. [similar]
EX: Coffee and toast cannot *compare with* eggs and bacon. [stating differences]

Differ from/differ with:

EX: Some British spelling *differs from* American. [not the same]

EX: She *differs with* the professor about the grade she received. [disagrees]

Different than/different from:

EX: His new girlfriend is quite *different than* the last one. [speech; American]
EX: The movie is quite *different from* the novel. [British]

NOTE: An online search will yield endless differences of opinion from dictionaries, style guides, professors and others about using *different than* vs *different from*. *Different from* seems to be preferred most often for British and American usage. *Different than* is justified as allowable by a few sources, but is more likely to be used by Americans or in conversation. The following sentence, however, appears to be grammatically correct:

EX: The author said that he would prefer to be different than boring.

Either/or/neither/nor:

EX: I have enough money left for *either* a sandwich *or* a movie. [correct]
EX: I have *neither* money *nor* time to go to the cinema. [correct]

EX: I have *neither* money *or* time to go to the cinema. [incorrect]
NOTE: Use either/or, or use neither/nor.

Identical to/identical with:

EX: Her dress is *identical to* mine. [correct]
EX: The names of many American places are *identical with* those in England. [incorrect]

MISUSED WORDS

Able vs capable:

    EX: He said that he is *able* to repair the car by Saturday afternoon. [ability]
    EX: The 1954 Austin Martin is *capable* of being restored. [capacity to do something]

Continual vs continuous:

    EX: The nearby construction work continually disturbed the lecture. [with occasional interruption]
    EX: The new clock ran continuously for five days; then stopped. [without interruption]

Easy vs easily:

    EX: She *easily* passed the exam, after studying day and night. [adverb]
    EX: She found the exam *easy* this time. [adjective]
    NOTE: [Another apology for more grammar terms. An adverb (e.g., easily) modifies a verb (e.g., passed), whereas an adjective (e.g., easy) modifies a noun or subject (e.g., exam). The adjective easy is changed into an adverb by using an *–ly* ending.]

Much vs many:

    EX: There is too *much* sugar in my tea. [Quantity cannot be counted; use *much*.]
    EX: How many teaspoons of sugar did you add? [The number can be counted, so use *many*, which refers to teaspoons, not sugar.]

    NOTE: [You may not say 'There is too *many* sugar in my tea' or 'How *much* teaspoons of sugar did you add?']. Use *much* if quantity cannot be counted; otherwise use *many*.

To vs for:

    EX: Can you send my grades *to* me? [direction]
    EX: Can you pick up my grades *for* me? [on my behalf]

<u>That vs which</u>:

Although the general view is that British grammar allows the use of *that* or *which* interchangeably and without commas, the difference between restrictive (essential) and non-restrictive (nonessential) clauses is recognized, and there is authority for using *that* for restrictive clauses and *which* (with a comma preceding it) for non-restrictive clauses for British grammar. The latter rule is recommended as the meaning of sentences will be clear in all cases, which is important in academic work. The former rule may cause ambiguity in certain cases or change the intended meaning of a sentence as illustrated by the following examples, but may be followed if the intended meaning is clear.

You may write a sentence either way—using *which* with commas or *that* without commas—but the meaning may not be the same. The difference may be too subtle for the average reader to notice; however, fat chance if the reader is your professor.

EX: The closest cinema, *which* has twelve screens, is fifteen minutes from my flat.
EX: The closest cinema *that* has twelve screens is fifteen minutes from my flat.

NOTE: [The first example states that the closest cinema is fifteen minutes from your flat, and the meaning is not changed by deleting the parenthetical 'which has twelve screens'. Therefore, the parenthetical is enclosed between commas.]

NOTE: [The second example contains a restrictive clause as it refers to the closest cinema that has twelve screens, which may not be the closest cinema (with a different number of screens).]

Although *which* is preferred for academic writing, this rule does not apply if its use changes the meaning of the sentence, as it would in the above example where commas are used to set off the parenthetical.

ACADEMIC: The cinema *which* I go to is fifteen minutes from my flat.

NON-ACADEMIC: The cinema *that* I go to is fifteen minutes from my flat.

The American rule is that *which* may only be used for things, whereas *that* may be used for either people or things. The British rule allows *that* to be used for people, in addition to things.

As indicated earlier, a comma is placed before *which* where it is part of a parenthetical expression, but not otherwise. A comma is not used before *that*.

>EX: The mall *which* I like the best is Bluewater.
>EX: This is the order in *which* the events will happen.
>EX: The question is *which* movie to see this weekend.

Was or Were:

Were is used in place of *was* in sentences which express something wishful, hypothetical or contrary to fact, even though this appears to violate the subject/verb agreement rule discussed below. See SUBJECT/VERB GREEMENT – PLURAL AND SINGULAR.

>EX: I wish *I was* living in Knightsbridge. [incorrect]
>NOTE: You might think that the above sentence is correct because both *I* and *was* are singular; the next example is correct even though *I* is singular and *were* is plural]

>EX: I wish *I were* living in Knightsbridge. [correct]
>EX: Things would be different if I was the Prime Minister.
>[incorrect]
>EX: Things would be different if I were the Prime Minister.
>[correct: hypothetical]

>EX: If I was rich I would buy a Rolls Royce. [incorrect]
>EX: If I were rich, I would buy a Rolls Royce [correct: because I am not rich]

Who or that:

Who refers to persons; *that* refers to groups (except groups of people) or inanimate objects (things). While *that* may be used in speech or informal writing, academic use requires the use of *who* when referring to persons.

EX: She is the person *who* won the lottery last week. [academic]

EX: She is the person *that* won the lottery last week. [speech]

Exception: *That* can refer to a person in very limited circumstances, as illustrated by the following example.

EX: *That* person took my book.

NOTE: [A class of people is considered as a thing (not a person); therefore, *that* should be used instead of *who*.]

EX: The class *that* receives the highest grades will win free tickets to the cinema.

OTHER WORD CHOICES

This/these and *that/those* may be used to refer to objects instead of using *the*. In addition, they will indicate whether the object is singular or plural, or near or distant in relation to the speaker, or may refer to time.

EX: *This* book is very expensive. [singular]
EX: *These* books are required reading. [plural]

EX: *This* pie is delicious. [near]
EX: Look at *that* couple in the last booth. [distant]

EX: *This* year I hope to buy a new car. [present]
EX: That was the year I lost a lot of money in the stock market. [past]

Everybody/everyone, somebody/someone, anybody/anyone, and *nobody/no one* are used differently in speech than academic writing.

EX: *Everybody* does it, so why can't I? [speech]
EX: *Everyone* will be required to take a final exam. [academic]

EX: *Somebody* took my book by mistake. [speech]
EX: *Someone* will be asked to take attendance each class. [academic]

EX: *Anybody* who likes animals is a friend of mine. [speech]
EX: *Anyone* who misses more than two classes will fail the course. [academic]

EX: *Nobody* should go out in this weather. [speech]
EX: *No one* should have to repeat this class. [academic]

NOTE: [*No one* is two separate words.]

Another word choice is whether to use or omit *that* in a sentence. *That* is frequently omitted in conversation, but usually retained in academic writing (even though the meaning is the same).

EX: The instructor said the test would be next Friday. [conversation]
EX: The instructor said *that* the test would be next Friday. [academic]

Programme/program is usually thought of as the difference between British and American spelling, which is correct if you are referring to a schedule of events, such as television shows or selections to be performed at a concert. However, *program* is used in the UK (as well as the US) to refer to computer applications.

Alternative may only be used when two choices are involved.

EX: We have the alternative of going to class, the cinema or the beach. [incorrect; there are more than two choices]

EX: We have the alternative of taking the final exam or repeating the class. [correct]

WORDS WITH MORE THAN ONE MEANING

Unlike many foreign languages, English contains an endless number of words with more than one meaning, many with multiple meanings.

EX: bank [place to deposit money]
EX: on the other bank [edge of a river]

EX: another round of drinks
EX: round the numbers to the nearest pound
EX: round of golf
EX: theatre in the round
EX: come round tomorrow morning

One meaning may be a noun, the other, a verb.

EX: Do not eat too much beef. [noun: cow]
EX: Stop beefing about it. [verb: complaining]

ETCETERA (ETC.)

Etc. is used in place of *and so forth*, and is placed at the end of a list to indicate that the list is *incomplete*. It should not be used at the end of a list that starts with *for example* or *such as*. Proper use does not include academic writing; instead, you should either include the whole list or use for *example* or *such as* for a partial list.

PARALLEL CONSTRUCTION

There are many types of parallel construction, but we will provide a few examples instead of explaining the complex rules. The first two examples illustrate the following rules: similar parts of a sentence should be written in the same way; events should be listed in the order of their occurrence. Shifting tenses is a type of parallel construction problem, discussed separately in the next section. Parallel construction also applies to lists, also discussed in another section. The words that need to be compared in the following examples are italicised.

Example 1:

INCORRECT: In the morning the students *studied*, and in the afternoon they *were taking* their exams.

CORRECT: In the morning the students *studied*, and in the afternoon they *took* their exams.

CORRECT: In the morning the students *were studying*, and in the afternoon they *were taking* their exams.

Example 2:

INCORRECT: I was afraid that I would take the class over, get a bad grade and fail the final exam.

CORRECT: I was afraid that I would fail the final exam, get a bad grade, and have to take the class over.

NOTE: [Events should be listed in the order they will occur.]

Example 3:

INCORRECT: The instructor agreed *that* she would be on time, *that* the exam would only take one hour, and she would finish grading before class was over. [Use *that* all three times or not at all; however, for academic work *that* must be used so it must be used all three times].

CORRECT: The instructor agreed *that* she would be on time, *that* the exam would only take one hour, and *that* she would finish grading before class was over.

Example 4:

INCORRECT: My resume *is* not only well-done but also *is* up-to-date.

CORRECT: My resume *is* not only well-done but also up-to-date.

Example 5:

INCORRECT: English classes are held on Monday, on Tuesday, Wednesday, and on Friday. [On should be used each time or only once, before Monday.]

CORRECT: English classes are held on Monday, Tuesday, Wednesday and Friday.

CORRECT: English classes are held on Monday, on Tuesday, on Wednesday and on Friday. [correct, but wordy]

NOTE: These two examples omit the Oxford comma (British style).

SHIFTING TENSES

Tense refers to a particular time of an action, generally in the past, present or future, although there are several additional types of tenses. You should not shift tenses in a sentence. Without giving you an explanation of the rules—boring—a few examples should suffice.

INCORRECT: During the lecture, I *fell* asleep and *drops* my notebook.

NOTE: [*Fell* is past tense; *drops* is present tense.]

CORRECT: During the lecture, I *fell* asleep and *dropped* my notebook.

NOTE: [Both *fell* and *dropped* are past tense.]

INCORRECT: When the professor *walks* into the room, everyone *will stand*.

NOTE: [*Walks* is present tense; *will stand* is future tense.]

CORRECT: When the professor *walks* into the room, everyone *stands*.

NOTE: [Both *walks* and *stands* are present tense.]

The rule against shifting tenses also applies to shifting from active to passive voice.

    EX: The professor read [active voice] the newspaper while the students were taking [passive voice] their final exams. [shifting voice]

EX: The professor read [active voice] the newspaper while the students took [active voice] their final exams. [consistent: active voice]

EX: The professor was reading [passive voice] the newspaper while the students were taking [passive voice] their final exams. [consistent: passive voice]

Generally, you should keep tenses the same for all sentences in the same paragraph.

SUBJECT/VERB AGREEMENT - PLURAL AND SINGULAR

The subject of a sentence must agree with the verb (the action). Not only that, they must agree in person and in number; otherwise you will have a sentence that grinds on the ears of the reader. The italicised words will help you focus on subject/verb agreement. Many students have difficulty applying this rule, especially if English is not their first language.

INCORRECT: Harold and Samantha *was* late for class.
CORRECT: Harold and Samantha *were* late for class.

INCORRECT: Several students *is* not going to graduate this year.
CORRECT: *Several* students *are* not going to graduate this year.

INCORRECT: The number of students *who are* going to fail is unfortunate.
CORRECT: The *number* of students *who is* going to fail is unfortunate.

INCORRECT: A few of us *wants* to go to Brighton this weekend.
CORRECT: A *few* of us *want* to go to Brighton this weekend.

INCORRECT: A box of donuts *were* delivered to the office.
CORRECT: A *box* of donuts was delivered to the office.
CORRECT: *Twelve* donuts *were* delivered to the office.

It is easy to make a mistake (subject/verb agreement) if the subject is not properly identified. In the above example the subject is *box*, not *donuts*, so a singular verb (*was*) must be used. In the next example the subject is *twelve*, which must be followed by a plural verb (*were*).

A parenthetical expression between the subject and the verb may mislead the writer and result in a sentence with an incorrect subject/verb agreement.

EX: Harold, as well as his girlfriend, *are* always late for class. [incorrect]
EX: Harold, as well as his girlfriend, *is* always late for class. [correct]

EX: Harold, together with some other students, are planning to spend this year's half term break at Brighton. [incorrect]
EX: Harold, together with some other students, is planning to spend this year's half term break at Brighton. [correct]

NOTE: [If you ignore the parentheticals in these sentences, it is clear that Harold is the subject and thus a singular verb (is) must be used for subject/verb agreement.]

EX: Harold and several other students are planning to spend this year's half term break at Brighton. [correct]

Collective words, such as team or group, require the use of singular verbs in American English. Either singular or plural verbs may be used in British English, although plural is more common, but be consistent in your choice throughout your essay.

EX: Parliament *has* finally voted on the budget for next year. [US]
EX: Parliament *have* finally voted on the budget for next year. [UK]

NOTE: [If you are not sure whether to use a singular or plural verb, you can always reword the sentence so that a plural verb may be used.]

EX: The members of Parliament *have* voted on the budget for next year.

In addition to consistency throughout your essay, you must be consistent within the same sentence in the use of singular or plural verbs for teams or groups, etc.

EX: The team was so distracted by the dog running around the field that they could not score any more goals. [incorrect]

EX: The team were so distracted by the dog running around the field that it could not score any more goals. [incorrect]

EX: The team were so distracted by the dog running around the field that they could not score any more goals. [UK: correct]
EX: The team was so distracted by the dog running around the field that it could not score any more goals. [US: correct]

Even if you have decided to use a plural verb to refer to a group, remember that a singular verb must be used to refer to a member of a group.

EX: Most of the actors *are* usually late for rehearsal.
EX: Each of the actors *is* paid on time.

Sometimes two words which are otherwise singular may be used together as a collective item, thus requiring a singular verb. However, they may also be used separately.

EX: Soup and salad *are* hardly my idea of a meal. [incorrect]
EX: Soup and salad *is* hardly my idea of a meal. [correct]
EX: Soup and salad *are* on my grocery shopping list. [correct]

NOUN/PRONOUN AGREEMENT - PLURAL AND SINGULAR

As stated above, pronouns—words that take the place of nouns (persons, places and things)—can be used to avoid repetition within a sentence, or even in a sentence that follows.

EX: The *book* was much too long and the *book* was not well-written.
EX: The *book* was much too long and *it* was not well-written.

EX: We went to see *Casablanca* last night. *It* is one of my favourite movies.

There are several points to remember concerning singular and plural nouns and pronouns.

First, it should be clear which noun the pronoun is referring to in order to avoid reader confusion and to apply the second rule (following these examples).

EX: He accidently hit his thumb with a hammer and *it* broke. [which one broke?]
EX: He broke his thumb when he accidently hit *it* with a hammer [clear].

EX: They should put extra cars on trains during holiday periods. [who are they?]

Second, you must use a singular pronoun for a singular noun, and a plural pronoun for a plural noun. Again, you must first determine which noun the pronoun refers to.

EX: I ordered a box of chocolates, but they never arrived. [incorrect: box is the subject, not chocolates; it (singular) should be used with box (singular)]
EX: When a person is late for the theatre *they* should wait for intermission. [incorrect]
EX: When a person is late for the theatre he or she should wait for intermission [correct]
EX: When people are late for the theatre *they* should wait for intermission. [correct]

The following words are singular and require a singular pronoun: *a person, anybody, anyone, each, everybody* and *nobody.*

EX: Each of the students *is* required to attend all lectures. [correct]
EX: Each of the students are required to attend all lectures. [incorrect: each is the subject, not students]

Third, a pronoun must agree in person with the subject that it refers to. What are we talking about? Person may be first person (I), second person (you) or third person (he, she, it, they).

EX: If *a person* wants to pass the course, *you* must study. [incorrect]

EX: If *a person* wants to pass the course, *they* must study. [incorrect]

EX: If *a person* wants to pass the course, *he or she* must study. [correct]

EX: If *you* want to pass the course, *you* must study. [correct]

Many writers, not just students, think (incorrectly) that they can avoid wordiness by using *their* in place of *his* or *her*, even though the subject is singular.

EX: If a student fails the final exam, *they* have to repeat the class. [incorrect]

EX: If a student fails the final exam, *he or she* will have to repeat the class. [correct]

If the writer is determined to use their, the sentence must be rewritten with a plural subject.

EX: He is like every *child* who has something to prove to *their* parents. [incorrect]

EX: He is like every *child* who has something to prove to *his or her* parents. [correct]

EX: He is like all *children* who have something to prove *to their* parents. [correct]

FAULTY PREDICATION

What the bloody hell is this, something wrong with my car? No, there is something wrong with your sentence. It is not logical because the subject and verb do not make any sense together and may (or may not) confuse the reader. The problem is that the subject of the sentence cannot carry out the action that the verb describes.

EX: The University believes that tuition should be increased next year.

NOTE: The University cannot believe; only its faculty or board members can.

81

EX: The reason Charlotte missed class was because she had a flat tire.

NOTE: [Charlotte's automobile or bicycle may have a flat tire, but not her.]

Although the last two examples are not likely to confuse the reader, they are not accurately worded.

FAULTY COORDINATION

Not more of this, you say. Briefly, faulty coordination is combining two clauses in an illogical manner. A few types of faulty coordination include combining clauses of unequal importance so that they seem equal, comparing absolute adjectives (words that cannot be compared) and making ambiguous comparisons.

EX: The professor paid £325,000 for his new home, and it has three floors. [clauses of unequal importance]

CORRECTED: The professor paid £325,000 for his new home, which has three floors.

EX: My most favourite film is *The King's Speech*. [incorrect comparison]

NOTE: [Only one film can be your favourite.]

EX: Claudia dislikes geometry more than Robert. [ambiguous comparison]

NOTE: [Does this mean that Claudia dislikes geometry more than she dislikes Robert, or that Claudia dislikes geometry more than Robert dislikes geometry?]

ACTIVE vs PASSIVE VOICE IN SENTENCES

Other than scientific writing, sentences should generally be written in active, not passive, voice. The difference depends on the whether the subject is acting or being acted upon.

If the subject of the sentence performs the action, it is active voice.

 EX: Harry *bought* a used car.
 EX: Two students *failed* the exam.

If the action is performed upon the subject of the sentence, it is passive voice.

 EX: The used car *was sold* to Harry.
 EX: One student *has been told* to repeat the class.

Stick to active sentences most of the time as they are usually more concise, interesting and to the point than passive ones, which are less directed to the reader. The use of passive voice is not necessarily incorrect, and may be used where appropriate. It is a question of style, not grammar. However, if you have too many passive sentences, try to rewrite them using active voice.

 EX (Passive): Dropping the last class on Fridays is being considered by the University.
 EX (Active):   The University is considering dropping the last class on Fridays.

RUN-ON SENTENCES

Run-on sentences (also called fused sentences) contain two or more complete thoughts, each of which could stand alone as a complete sentence. The thoughts are strung together either without any intervening punctuation or are incorrectly separated by a comma. The former may be corrected in one of three ways: (1) making separate sentences out of each thought; (2) inserting a semicolon; or (3) inserting a conjunction (and, but, for, or, nor, so, yet). The latter may also be corrected in three ways: (1) making separate sentences out of each thought; (2) using a semicolon instead of a comma, or (3) leaving the comma in place, and inserting a conjunction (and, but, for, or, nor, so, yet) after it.

Most run-on sentences have only two complete thoughts, although sometimes they have more, and on occasion run on and on, and on, unfortunately a writing style favoured by many students.

Another unofficial style of some students is to intersperse several run-on sentences with numerous sentence fragments, which of course are not complete thoughts. This is where the writing often becomes wordy, vague and rambling, indicating a lack of focus.

WORDY SENTENCES AND PHRASES

Lengthy sentences and paragraphs display lack of writing skills and often lack of effort. Long-winded sentences frequently ramble on and on, filled with too many ideas or unrelated material. Redundancy and run-on sentences can also contribute to wordiness.

You are not getting paid by the word, like the pulp fiction writers in the early part of the twentieth century, not that they were paid very much.

- Get to the point. [Stop beating about the bush.]
- Say what you have to say and stop. [Put a sock in it.]
- Start the next sentence. [Move on.]
- Cut out wordy expressions. [Be concise.]

You can start improving by cutting out wordy expressions. Here are just a few examples.

WORDY	IMPROVEMENTS
A small number of	a few
At this point in time	at this time
Based on the fact that	because
During the course of	during
Engaged in the study of	studying
In the majority of instances	usually
In the very near future	soon
On a weekly basis	weekly
Take into consideration	consider
This is a subject that	this subject

REDUNDANCY

Related to wordiness is redundancy, which can contribute to wordiness. Redundancy is saying the same thing more than once by using repetitive or similar words or phrases whose use is duplicative or overlaps in meaning. Look for it in your work and delete. A few examples follow.

EX: The auditorium is large in size.
NOTE: [Large denotes size].

EX: Each and every time I take the bus I am late.
NOTE: [Each and every mean the same thing].

EX: My dissertation contains only true facts.
NOTE: [A fact is something that is true].

EX: New innovations are announced every week.
NOTE: [An innovation by definition is something new].

Examples of redundancy using duplicative descriptions:

EX: Four o'clock is the time of day when afternoon tea is typically served.

NOTE: [Using time of day is redundant as four o'clock is a time of day.]

EX: The substitute instructor who was always complaining about the amount of work was fired after several classes because of his constant complaints about his workload.

NOTE: [This is redundant because it says the same thing twice.]

EX: I will not repeat myself again; attend all classes or you will not pass the course.

NOTE: [*Repeat* and *again* are redundant.]

EX: Contractions should not be used in academic work unless used in a quotation that reflects exactly what the speaker said, word for word.

NOTE: [*Exactly* and *word for word* are redundant.]

Some cases of redundancy will not be so obvious, but (unlike the examples above) the sentence may sound a bit awkward.

EX: I think the company will accept my novel because it previously published similar novels before. [Either *previously* or *before* should be deleted.]

If you repeat what you say for emphasis, the result is most likely redundancy.

WORDS AND OTHER THINGS TO AVOID

Get: *Get* and *got* have several meanings and are quite often used in conversation, but should be avoided in academic writing if another word can be substituted. If not, rewrite the sentence.

EX: I *got* a terrible grade on the last exam.
EX: I *received* a terrible grade on the last exam.

EX: Did you *get* what I said?
EX: Did you *understand* what I said?

EX: Have you *got* a budget for your film project?
EX: Have you *made* a budget for your film project?

EX: You must get on the train for London before noon.
EX: You must board the train for London before noon.

EX: The restaurant will cancel the reservation if she does not get there by noon.
EX: The restaurant will cancel the reservation if she does not arrive by noon.

EX: *Get* out of my way.
NOTE: [This example probably requires rewriting.]

EX: *Step aside*; you are in my way.

The: If you start a sentence with the word *the*, delete it and see if the meaning of the sentence is still clear. If not, put it back.

EX: The students are usually late for the first class on Monday mornings.

EX: Students are usually late for the first class on Monday mornings. [same meaning]

NOTE: [Certain names (including buildings, geographical and plural geographical names) must be preceded by *the*, wherever they appear in a sentence.]

EX: It was cold and windy the last time I took a boat ride on the Thames.

EX: The Cayman Islands are a favourite vacation choice.
EX: I would like to go to the Cayman Islands next year.

<u>There are</u>: Try to avoid starting a sentence with 'there are', and get to the thought or action.

EX: There are millions of people who would like to win the lottery.
EX: Millions of people would like to win the lottery. [better]

Shorten your sentences by cutting out extraneous clauses that delay getting to the point; they are really filler material, discussed later. However, do not write only short sentences as you must vary their length for style.

EX: As you may know, the university intends to increase tuition next term.
EX: The university intends to increase tuition next term. [concise]

Sentences may also be shortened by condensing them into fewer words which have the same meaning. This is done by cutting out words that are not needed; the missing words can be implied by the reader. The examples that follow show the words in brackets which can be deleted without a change in meaning.

EX: The professor's car looks older than my uncle's [car].

EX: How many subjects did you take last term? [Last term I took] Four [subjects].

Another way to write shorter sentences is to place a word that modifies another word in front of (instead of after) it.

87

EX: a seminar *that is long*
EX: a *long* seminar

On the other hand, you may do the opposite for emphasis or a change of meaning.

EX: The use of *aluminium* cookware has caused health concerns.
EX: The use of cookware *made of aluminium* has caused health concerns.

Clichés:

Be careful not only to avoid clichés, but also cliché adjectives, which say the same thing twice:

absolute certainty
actual facts
close proximity
free gifts
new beginning
unexpected surprise

NOTE: [The foregoing are also examples of redundancy (e.g., something cannot be a surprise, by definition, unless it is unexpected).]

NOTE: [A *gift* by definition is something that is *free*. However, beyond the world of academic writing we know that many gifts come with strings (restrictions) attached and that any 'free gift' offered on TV requires payment of shipping and handling. As an economist once said, 'If it's free, it's too expensive'.]

Negating adverbs:

These are adverbs that minimise, neutralise or nullify the words they modify, thus defeating the intended meaning.

EX: somewhat lethal [it is either lethal or not]
EX: fairly disgusting [fairly de-emphasizes disgusting]

MISSING ARTICLES

Unfortunately, here is a bit more about grammar. You do not need Miss Marple or Hercule Poirot to find your missing articles; a grammar check should do the job. The most common articles are *the* (a definite article), which refers to a specific subject; and *a* or *an* (indefinite articles), which refer to non-specific subjects. Although the rules generally refer to nouns, which may be either things or ideas, we will use the term 'subjects' and 'nouns' interchangeably. *The*, *a* and *an* are more frequently omitted from the work of students whose first language is not English, whereas the choice between *a* or *an* may give anyone a headache.

Before we go on, it should be pointed out that there are two types of rules which must be considered in deciding whether to use or omit articles: (1) whether the noun is countable or uncountable, in the case of *the*, *a* or *an*; and (2) the sound (vowel or consonant) of the noun as pronounced, in the case of *a* or *an*.

Countable nouns may be either singular or plural and refer to things which can be counted, such as apple (apples), book (books), class (classes) and university (universities), etc.

An article or a possessive word (e.g., her, my) must be used with a singular countable noun.

    EX: My girlfriend wants to buy house in Kensington. [incorrect: article is missing]
    EX: My girlfriend wants to buy *a* house in Kensington. [correct: countable]
    EX: I prefer to buy *the* house that is for sale across the street. [correct: countable]

Although an article should not be used with an uncountable noun, an article may be allowed where the uncountable noun is used in a countable context.

    EX: I would like a sugar in my coffee. [incorrect: uncountable]
    EX: I would like a teaspoon of sugar in my coffee. [correct: countable, because the article (a) modifies teaspoon, not sugar]

EX: Give me a coffee. [speech or informal; not academic]

NOTE: Coffee may be considered countable in this
sentence because the intended subject is a cup (of coffee),
but more appropriately should be limited to speech.

To make things more complicated, there are situations when
none of the articles (*the*, *a,* or *an*) should be used. No article is
used for uncountable nouns (e.g., sugar), sports (e.g., soccer),
or things in general (e.g., inflation); or for plural countable nouns.

EX: *The* inflation is worse than last year. [incorrect:
uncountable]
EX: Inflation is worse than last year. [correct]
EX: The inflation rate is worse than last year. [correct:
inflation is used as an adjective, not a noun]

EX: I don't have enough money for a vacations this year.
[incorrect: plural countable]
EX: I don't have enough money for vacations this year.
[correct: plural countable]

The article *the* or a possessive word used in place of *the* (e.g.,
her, my) must be used with a singular uncountable noun or plural
countable noun when referring to a specific subject, but not
something in general.

EX: We are almost out of water. [correct: general]
EX: We are almost out of the water. [incorrect: general]
EX: We are almost out of the water that you bought last
week. [correct: specific]

You should not start a sentence with *the* and say 'The soccer is
on every Saturday at seven o'clock' instead of 'Soccer is on
every Saturday at seven o'clock'. *The* is usually not used with
the name of a country (e.g., England, Italy), but this is not always
true (e.g., the United Kingdom, the United States).

In some sentences, the inclusion or omission of *the* is optional
with uncountable nouns.

EX: I especially like the snow at Christmas.
EX: I especially like snow at Christmas.

There are a few more rules concerning the use of the word *the*. When referring to institutions such as a church, college, hospital or university in a general way, *the* is not used; it is only used when referring to a specific institution or place, whether or not its name is stated.

EX: If I save enough money, I will go to university next year. [general]

EX: If I win the lottery, I will go to Cambridge University next year. [specific]

EX: The church is next to the clock tower in the town centre. [specific, though the name is not mentioned]

The is also used when referring to a specific place.

EX: Let's go to the cinema after we go to the library. [correct]

EX: Let's go to the cinema after the library. [better worded if 'we go to' is deleted]

EX: I will go to the doctor in the morning, then to the mall. [correct]

There are also differences between British and American usage.

EX: He was hit by a car and will be in hospital for a few days. [UK]

EX: He was hit by a car and will be in *the* hospital for a few days. [US]

Since it seems that almost every grammar rule has exceptions, we will say that *generally* every countable noun requires an article (e.g., an apple, a book, the ticket-if referring to a specific ticket). Students whose writing frequently omits required articles (*the*, *a,* or *an*) may want to review the countable nouns in their work in search of missing articles. You should note that the plural of countable nouns (e.g., apples, books and tickets) do not require articles.

The basic rule, as clarified below, is that *an* is used before words that begin with a vowel (a,e,i,o,u); *a* is used before words that begin with a consonant (all letters except vowels). That may sound easy, but it is not that simple. The problem is that the rule depends on the 'sound' of the word, not its spelling.

Examples with *a*	Examples with *an*
A ticket	An idea
A building	An office
A country	An empire

We will now restate the basic rule—more accurately: *an* is used before words that begin with a vowel (a,e,i,o,u) sound; *a* is used before words that begin with a consonant sound.

Examples with *a*	Examples with *an*
A unique design	An unusual design
A half hour	An hour
A horrible flight	An escape

NOTE: 'Unique' is pronounced with a hard sound (like a consonant), and thus requires *a*. Unlike the word half, the *h* is silent when 'hour' is pronounced, and therefore *an* must be used with hour. *An* is also required to be used with 'escape' because the vowel (e) is silent.

If an adjective modifies a noun, the above rule applies to the adjective that modifies the noun instead of the noun; the article is placed before the adjective.

Examples with *a*	Examples with *an*
A difficult exam	An easy exam
A strong headache	An endless headache
A large apple	An apple
A box of apples	An order of apple pie
A dozen eggs	An egg

NOTE: You may say a difficult exam, but not a exam; you may say an easy exam, but not a easy exam.

Remember that *the* is a definite article which refers to specific items, whereas *a* or *an* refer to items in general.

> EX: Bring me *the* book I bought yesterday. [definite: a specific book]

EX: Bring me *a* magazine from the store. [indefinite: any magazine]

EX: Bring me *an* Italian cookbook from the bookstore. [indefinite: any Italian cookbook]

EX: A policeman came to the university yesterday. [indefinite: he is not yet identified]

EX: The policeman questioned everyone. [definite: if this follows the preceding sentence we know who is being referred to as he is already being talked about]

Even though the meaning is basically the same, the choice of article may depend on how a sentence is worded.

EX: I had *a* hard time with grammar last term.

EX: *The* hardest time I had last term was with grammar.

HOTCHPOTCH

Hotchpotch, originally a legal term and later used for stew, has come to mean a mismatch of items or ideas. Although not a grammatical term, which we have attempted to keep to a minimum, we will use hotchpotch to describe a paragraph that contains unending run-on sentences and unclear ideas, interspersed with sentence fragments, often with some redundancy thrown in for good measure. Reading such work will likely evoke a few choice words from the person marking the work, who is likely paid a mere pittance for reading such codswallop but cannot under university rules afford to tell the writer to get stuffed. If you have read this far, you have no doubt learned how to avoid such a disaster.

LOGICAL WRITING

Your presentation must be in a logical order and move from one paragraph to the next without a break in transition of language or thought. If it does not, start rewriting; it may require a lot of work but do not stop until you get it right. The same applies to sentences, which must move smoothly from one to the next.

Always be careful when you move a sentence or paragraph to another location in your essay as other changes may be necessary, and sometimes require substantial rewriting. If you add material to a well-written paragraph, it may interrupt the flow of words and require further rewriting. If you do not think that any rewriting is necessary after moving words or sentences around, read the sentence or paragraph again to be sure.

However is used to limit or contradict something previously stated, but has a side effect of interrupting the flow of thought for the reader. Its placement in the sentence (beginning, middle or end) will affect the degree of disruption, which may be less if placed at the end. When placed at the beginning, *however* interrupts the preceding sentence, either by minimizing it or by contrast. Because *however* disrupts the flow of thought it should be used sparingly. If your work is generously loaded with *however*, get rid of most of them and count how many are left.

QUEUE PROPERLY

This means to wait your turn in line and not crowd in front of others. The following examples will illustrate a similarity in grammar, and more particularly word order.

INCORRECT: Me and my sister went to the cinema last night.

NOTE: This may seem accurate to you if you stood in line in front of your sister, especially if you paid for both tickets, but it is not correct grammar.

CORRECT: My sister and I went to the cinema last night.

INCORRECT: 'Get well soon, from me and Anna.'
CORRECT: 'Get well soon, from Anna and me.'

DID YOU WRITE WHAT YOU MEANT TO SAY?

What you intended to say is in your head and may not have made it on paper the same way. The reader will be the judge of what you actually said. When you proofread and edit your work, you may find that a sentence does not quite express the thought you intended. This may require rewriting or perhaps merely changing the word order if words are not in the right place. Sometimes the problem is just poor sentence construction, incorrect grammar or making changes without being careful.

EX: I will produce a trailer for my film <u>as it since</u> does not cost that much. [incorrect]

NOTE: The sentence will be correct if either 'since' or 'as it' is deleted. In this sentence, it is possible that the writer started to write the sentence one way, then changed his or her mind and reworded it without deleting the words no longer necessary. This type of error may also happen during rewriting.

If you intentionally say one thing and mean another (possibly the opposite) you are using irony, which should be used cautiously in academic work so as not to give the reader the impression that you do not know what you are talking (writing) about. Other mistakes (such as using the wrong word) do not involve irony, and unintentionally say the opposite of what you intended.

EX: I sent my manuscript to an agent to help me get it published, and am meeting with him next week to see if he is on bored.

NOTE: The intended meaning is to say that the writer hopes that the agent will be on board to help get his novel published. Unfortunately 'bored', which means unenthusiastic or uninterested, has a negative connotation.

CAN YOU IMPROVE?

Yes, of course you can improve. You have made it this far. You are in university and expected to deliver academic quality writing. If you follow the advice in this book, instead of turning in your assignment after a single grammar/spell check and cursory proofreading, the quality of your work is bound to improve. Do not be discouraged if you find many mistakes after you review your work for the first time. This is only the first draft and the initial goal is to put your ideas down in writing, not to perfect them. The key to good writing is rewriting, usually several times. You can succeed if you are willing to put in the effort. After you have polished your work to an academic level, do not forget to review it again to be sure that it complies with all of the requirements of your assignment. Keep deadlines in mind and do not run up to close to them.

HOW TO START WRITING

Obviously you should read the instructions first, including any style requirements of the university. Next you should make a list or an outline of what you will cover in your academic paper. The instructions may include certain topics or questions that must be covered, discussed or analysed; do what is asked and do not omit anything. Think about what you are going to say before you start writing. You may find it necessary to do some research before you start.

The topic of your academic paper may be one assigned to you or one of your own choosing. In either case, you should grab the reader's attention in the first few sentences. This is part of creating a good impression and will generate interest in your paper. At the other end, your conclusion should be well written and supported by the contents of your essay.

You may just want to just jump in and plough through the whole thing and fine-tune it later. After all, if you stop to fix every little thing as you write the first draft, you will never get to the end, the term will be over and everyone else will be on holiday. Even if you proceed in this manner, you may want to fix any spelling mistakes—usually underlined in red by software programs—as you go along. Other students may prefer the opposite approach, correcting spelling, grammar and usage during the writing of the first draft. Those who take the latter approach should not try to improve each sentence or paragraph by rewriting them while correcting the first draft. If you want, you can highlight words or sentences that you want to review or rewrite later in order to keep moving forward.

STYLE OF WRITING

The style of one's writing covers many aspects

- Sentence structure
- Variation in length of sentences and paragraphs
- Variety in types of sentence patterns, including use of parenthetical expressions
- Clarity, which also requires correct punctuation and word order presentation
- Brevity, which sticks to essentials

- Avoidance of run-on sentences, redundant words and repetitive descriptions or sentences
- Accuracy of information, backed up with appropriate references
- Avoiding vague generalisations
- Presenting material in a logical order
- Keeping the flow of the material moving
- Conforming to academic standards of writing

PROOFREAD, EDIT AND CRITICISE YOUR OWN WORK

Ask yourself these two questions after you have read your work; then consider the list that follows.

Would you show it to a prospective employer as a writing sample?

How much money, if any, would you pay someone else for work of this quality?

- Does the formatting look great?
- Do sentences and paragraphs vary in length?
- Have you done a spell check?
- Have you done a grammar check?
- Have you proofread your work from a hard copy (not on a computer screen)?
- Does each sentence clearly say what you are trying to convey?
- Have you eliminated unnecessary words?
- Have you eliminated redundant words or phrases?
- Have you replaced repeated words with synonyms?
- Should you change the word order to improve any sentences?
- Does your work have continuity?
- Are your sentences and paragraphs in a logical order?
- Do the first few sentences grab the reader's attention?
- Does your work end with a summary or conclusion?
- Have you followed the instructions for your essay?

PROOFREADING, EDITING AND REWRITING

Proofreading consists of reviewing your work for spelling mistakes, typos, proper capitalisation, extra spaces, grammar errors and punctuation mistakes, as well as inconsistencies in language, spelling, formatting and word choice errors. It is the first thing and the last thing that you should do, with some additional proofreading in between (after each rewrite or at least each major rewrite).

Editing is reading your essay to improve it, and involves rewriting, which takes into account style, readability and many other things discussed above (e.g., variation in length of sentences and paragraphs, eliminating unnecessary words). Although not typically mentioned as part of editing, it should include a review of the work to be certain that all requirements of your assignment have been met and that no material has been omitted.

Proofreading and editing (including rewriting), are intertwined but should be approached separately in reviewing, correcting and polishing your academic work. In addition, each of them should be broken down into several steps. Some software programs check spelling and grammar separately; others check both at the same time. For each of the following steps, read through your entire material and focus only on that step.

First, check your spelling, and whether you have spelt the same words consistently throughout. As part of this step, check capitalisation for correctness and uniformity.

Second, do a grammar check, which may require minimal rewriting; save anything major for later; highlight in yellow (or some other colour) for easy reference. Look out for word choice errors (e.g., words spelt the same or with the same sound but which have different meanings).

Third, check the formatting for presentation and consistency as discussed earlier in this book. As part of this step, look for proper use and consistency of italics (e.g., book and movie titles). During this process look out for missing articles (*the*, *a* or *an*).

Fourth, move on to the editing and rewriting phase, but remember that after each major draft or rewrite, spelling and grammar checks must be repeated as strange things sometimes happen during rewriting, especially when text is moved around.

Note: Rewriting is part of the editing process; do not rewrite (other than making minor changes or corrections) while you are doing a grammar or spell check.

Do not forget: you must do final proofreading (after your final edit) from a hard copy, not a computer screen.

EDITING AND REWRITING – DO IT MORE THAN ONCE

As we have already stated, editing and rewriting does not mean checking spelling, grammar and formatting; you have already done that as part of the proofreading process. The purpose of editing, which is primarily rewriting, is to improve your work. Try to keep in mind all those things that affect your writing style as you go over your material.

Editing, like proofreading, is more effective if divided into several steps. Start by reading through the whole essay or document solely to see if you have varied long and short sentences and paragraphs. After making any changes, go back and read your material again, this time focusing on content, rewording or rewriting where appropriate. As part of this process, try to delete unnecessary words and shorten sentences; alternatively, do a separate read through of your material solely to delete unnecessary words and shorten sentences. You may want to do this more than once.

Each time after you rewrite, or at least after a major rewrite, you must do another spell check and grammar check; in addition to correcting any errors, you may notice ways to improve the work as you go through it. After that, you can repeat the process until you are satisfied, or run out of time. It is also a good idea to save your file with a different name each time you make substantial changes. This will be helpful if you change your mind later on and want to restore some words or sentences that you deleted earlier.

If you find it necessary to change a specific word throughout your work (such as a name or place), you can use the find and replace function of your software, but do so carefully. You can click the button to find and replace a word everywhere in a document at once, but this sometimes yields strange results here and there; it is safer to make such changes one at a time, but again, this is up to you.

For a final edit read though your essay for readability and the quality of your work, as well as ascertaining that all required material is included in the essay. If you are satisfied, do a final proofreading (spelling and grammar).

Some students prefer to work only on the computer screen; others from a hard copy. Each student should decide what works best, but you should definitely do your final editing and proofreading from a hard copy or you will invariably miss something. Either way you will need to rewrite more than once to achieve high-quality academic work.

One last reminder: Be sure to check the settings in your word processing program to be sure that the language is set to British English (unless you intend to use American English) and that the spelling and grammar checks are not off. If you are using Microsoft Word, you should also go to the <u>Review tab</u> at the top of the screen, select the <u>Spelling & Grammar</u> menu and then click on <u>Options</u> to see what functions it will perform in reviewing your work. The default is usually set on <u>Grammar Only</u>, which will correct spelling but not do a very thorough grammar check. Instead, select <u>Grammar and Style</u>; you will notice quite a difference in suggested changes and corrections, but you (not the software program) will have to decide which ones are appropriate.

FILLER MATERIAL

This means padding your work with extra words or phrases that add nothing to the content, but are merely to fill up space and meet the minimum number of words required for your assignment. If you are short thirty-five words out of a required five-hundred, okay, go ahead and plug in a few extra words here and there, but avoid redundant words. Extra words should be placed in a sentence where they will not disrupt the existing word flow.

WAFFLE PARAGRAPHS

Waffle means to go on and on, whilst saying nothing useful or important. This is where the writer rambles on with generalisations and displays only superficial knowledge of the subject, or does not delve into the question or topic that is to be discussed. Such writing is vague and will bore the reader—your instructor.

EX: In this essay, which is a requirement of my film business class during the fall term, I will discuss the various legal aspects, including but not limited to copyright issues, encountered from time to time in the motion picture industry by those persons interested or engaged in the acquisition of screenplays or other literary properties for the purpose of producing and distributing feature-length motion pictures, as well as TV syndication and the exploitation of other intellectual property rights and many other things.

NOTE: [The above example, in addition to saying nothing useful, is filler material. It is also an example of a poor introduction to the material that is to follow. It does however, tip off the reader to grab a coffee and not expect too much.]

USE AN AXE TO TIGHTEN UP YOUR WORK

This is an arbitrary rule of thumb, which you can modify or ignore, but it will teach you discipline if you apply it. Let's start big. Calculate how many words equal ten percent of your work; if you are less ambitious, you can use five percent. If your work is 3,000 words, for example, ten percent is 300 words. Your task is to start at the beginning of your masterpiece and chop out 300 unnecessary words. If you have not reached the end by the time you have removed 300 words, keep on deleting. On the other hand, if you have reached the end without meeting your goal you should start over (unless you cannot tighten your sentences any further). Another way to do this is to start be deleting 100 words; then delete another 100, etc. You can count the number of words deleted by using the word count feature of your word processing program, comparing the word count before and after deletions.

If the result puts you below the minimum required number of words for your assignment, you will have to add more content.

The point is that in the meantime you will have tightened up your work and made it much better. An alternative is to just go through your work and eliminate as many words as possible instead on focusing on a percent. However, do not just delete words to meet a numerical goal; eliminate unnecessary words, sentence by sentence. In the process of deleting words, you may find it necessary to make minor changes along the way, which is acceptable as long as you do not start adding unnecessary words.

BREVITY

Let's start with the introduction. Do not begin by telling the reader at length what you are going to write about—just start writing, with a brief description that makes the topic clear to the reader. We have seen students' work that expands what they are going to discuss to a full page.

> EX: The purpose of my essay, which I will discuss at length in the body of this paper, is the future of the music industry, taking into account the many changes that are currently taking place or may take place in the future. [extremely long-winded]

> EX: This essay will discuss the future of the music industry. [concise]

> NOTE: Your introduction need not be limited to one sentence as in the above 'extreme' example; it may be several sentences, but should be concise and focused.

As you edit your sentences, delete unnecessary words, but not important information or words, especially those that will change the meaning of the sentence. You will often be able to shorten sentences by rewriting those that begin with *that, which,* or *who.* Although you need to shorten sentences by making them tighter, remember that you still need some long sentences for variety.

> EX: The temporary lecturer, who recently came from Scotland, gave us exams that could never be finished in the allotted time.

> EX: The Scottish lecturer never gave us enough time to finish our exams.

EX: The new block of flats, which will have ten floors, is under construction and may be finished by the end of the year.

EX: Construction of the ten floor block of flats may be finished by year-end.

REORGANIZING WORD ORDER

Sometimes in editing or rewriting your work you will notice that a particular sentence does not work or does not say what you are trying to convey or does not make much sense. You may be able to rearrange the word order instead of rewriting the whole sentence or deleting it. As mentioned above a sentence can be worded several different ways by merely changing the word order—one way to achieve variety in your writing. However, be careful; changing the word order may result in a change of meaning or emphasis.

EX: I have a few books in my flat. [positive: some books]
EX: I have few books in my flat. [negative: not very many books]

Possibly a sentence should go somewhere else in your work; maybe in the same paragraph. Once it is moved you are not through; read the sentence carefully to see if it fits smoothly into its new location. Revision of the moved sentence may be required, as well as the paragraph in which it is placed. As you read your work—carefully and methodically—see which sentences you can improve, even those that are not problem sentences. The same considerations apply to the order of sentences within a paragraph; rearrange them if they are not in logical order.

Although you can word the same sentence more than one way, and change the word order for variety, be careful. If you do not place an adverb (such as *just*, for example) close to the word it is intended to modify, the sentence may mean something other than what you intended.

EX: Harry *just* went to the mall to buy some new socks.
EX: Harry went to the mall *just* to buy some new socks.

NOTE: [The first example says that Harry just left for the mall; the second says that he went to the mall only to buy some new socks. There is clearly a difference in meaning.]

Another word of caution about word order: be careful where you put the word *only* in your sentences, as it can change the meaning.

EX: I *only* wear my jacket when I go to the bank to borrow money.
EX: I wear my *only* jacket when I go to the bank to borrow money.

NOTE: [The first example is ambiguous as it implies that I own one jacket, but I may own more than one; the second makes it clear that I only own one jacket.]

EX: The president of the bank only drives his car to work when the chauffeur is sick.

NOTE: [This example implies that the president of the bank owns one car, but it is likely that someone of his stature owns more than one car.]

The average reader will probably understand what the writer is trying to say, but a more careful reader will find ambiguity in some of the sentences in the examples.

EX: The president of the bank only drives one of his cars to work when the chauffeur is sick. [clear: he has more than one car but we do not care which one he drives]

EX: The president of the bank only drives his Rolls Royce to work when the chauffeur is sick.

NOTE: [Although it is not clear if the president of the bank owns more than one car, it is not important as we know which car he drives to work when the chauffeur is sick—the Rolls Royce.]

AMBIGUITY AND CONFUSION

The meaning of a sentence may vary or be ambiguous depending on the placement or absence of commas or hyphens, as well as word order. Apart from punctuation or word order, poor wording of a sentence may cause ambiguity or confusion. In some cases, the reader will understand the intended meaning of a poorly worded sentence even though it is inaccurate as worded. This may be common for newspaper headlines, but is not acceptable for academic writing.

> EX: Investors Will Hear Stock Market Talk at Noon. [the stock market cannot talk]
> EX: The police have begun to run down stolen bicycles. [crash into or find?]

MISTAKES FREQUENTLY FOUND IN STUDENT ESSAYS

Most of the problems frequently found in university students' work have already been discussed in this book, but a summary of common mistakes follows.

The quality of university student academic writing varies from excellent to poor, with much good work in between. In many cases the quality of otherwise good content is diminished by the frequency of mistakes found in the work, which could have easily been fixed with a little effort—spelling and grammar checks, as well as some editing and rewriting. If you are using Microsoft Word, it underlines spelling errors in red; possible grammar problems are sometimes, but not always, underlined in green. Yet the work of many students indicates that they have ignored what should have been clear warnings. However, relying strictly on such grammar checks is an invitation for trouble, or worse. Unfortunately, grammar-checking programs sometimes fail to disclose problems, ones often revealed by a careful reading of your work from a printed copy. On the other hand, this failure may be the result of using the wrong settings in the grammar-check program. See EDITING AND REWRITING – DO IT MORE THAN ONCE above.

In far too many cases, students do not follow instructions, mostly by omitting parts of the assignment or glossing over topics in general terms rather than discussing or analysing them. This happens more often than one might think. After an essay is finished, the instructions should be reviewed again to see if anything has been left out.

Many students start with an extremely long opening paragraph, or a short introduction followed by a lengthy paragraph. This creates an initial impression with the reader that is not favourable. Lengthy paragraphs should be divided into shorter paragraphs, whether or not it is easy to do. As stated above, many students have apparently never heard of the semicolon while others cannot use enough commas or frequently make the wrong choice between commas and semicolons. Others, or the same ones, seem partial to run-on sentences, or in their haste to get done throw in awkward sentences and move on. When it comes to paragraphs and run-on sentences, students must learn to be brief and concise; avoid filler material and redundancy.

Lack of consistency is one of the most frequent problems found in student work, though not a problem for most students. Names of persons are sometimes capitalised, other times not, or merely the first name (and not the surname) is capitalised. The names of movies and books are mistreated in similar fashion, often with italics missing or quotation marks used instead of italics. Different spacing and font sizes, mentioned in the next paragraph, are other examples of inconsistency.

Formatting is not a problem for most students, but others will use different spacing between paragraphs or no spacing, and occasionally different font sizes in the same paragraph or even in the same sentence. Such things should pop out as you read over your material. These problems sometimes result from cutting and pasting (from another source) and make your work look sloppy.

Although they do not occur very often in student work, other things to avoid are double-spacing, using bold font throughout the essay, and even worse, centre spacing (which immediately creates a negative impression).

In using or omitting articles (*the*, *a* or *an*) you need to remember that there are two types of rules that must be considered: (1) the sound (vowel or consonant) of the noun and (2) whether the noun is countable or uncountable. This is frequently more of a problem for students whose first language is not English.

CONCLUSION

That is enough about grammar, punctuation and editing. If you have finished reading this book in its entirety, you should be able to improve your writing skills and level of academic work. However, it will require some effort on your part: writing, proofreading (including grammar and spell checks), editing and rewriting; all should be done more than once. Before you start writing, read the instructions (including any style requirements of the university) and organize your thoughts about what to include in your essay. When you have finished your final editing and proofreading, put your essay aside for a few days; then read it again for the last time, preferably in a comfortable chair in a nice coffeehouse. By now, you should have fixed all of the problems with your work, so your focus this time will be on readability. Hopefully no more changes will be required and you will be pleased with your grade.

62114518R00069

Made in the USA
Charleston, SC
01 October 2016